Learn Chinese Without WRITING

Unspoken Rules of Chinese Characters

Develop Visual Skills to Learn Chinese

W.Q. BLOSH

Learn Chinese Without Writing
Unspoken Rules of Chinese Characters
W.Q. BLOSH

FIRST EDITION

Written and designed by W.Q. BLOSH

Email: wqblosh@gmail.com

ISBN: 978-981-09-7669-9 (Paperback)

Printed by IngramSparks

PREFACE

Put this book down if you are hoping to learn pronunciation, reading, vocabulary ... because you are not going to learn all these in this book! This book just wants to share with you how to 'see' to learn Chinese.

Seeing

When we fall in love with something or somebody, often sight has a role to play initially. Seeing could be about aesthetics ... appreciating the beauty or more importantly ... seeing is about developing our sense of something so we can understand it better.

Many underestimated the fact that Chinese is very different from other languages and requires a radical approach to learn it, especially when it is learnt as a foreign language. Learners without a stimulating learning environment where exposure to Chinese characters sensitise them to the intricacies of Chinese characters, may lag behind in characters recognition. They are in need of guidance on what to look out for, where to focus their attention and how to distinguish these characters.

Perceptual Learning

Have you ever wondered why experts are able to quickly and effortlessly sift out what is critical and relevant? This is the result of perceptual learning. Experts are able to deal with information more efficiently and effectively than novices because they are able to **see patterns and underlying structure** in the information. Novices are essentially blind to patterns that the experts have come to see immediately.

Native Chinese are able to extract meaningful clues from characters instantaneously. They seem to have radar eyes that can scan for the right information. Such visual acuity is one of the more challenging hurdles non-native learners face.

Natives view the sights and sounds streaming through their senses as meaningful information as their brains provided the meaning to seeing connections. Learning is a result of making associations between the sights observed.

Perceptual learning is such a basic skill that we forget we have it. It is what we use as children to make distinctions between similar-looking alphabets. In the early stages of learning, full attention is needed to integrate all the isolated circuits in the brain. Once the skill is mastered, performance is automatic. It is a kind of learning that humans of all ages do naturally given the right learning opportunities.

We believe that perceptual skills are trainable. We use them every time we try to learn new materials. Once our eyes—or other senses—have mastered these subtle perceptual nuances, we can focus on putting such knowledge to work. The beauty of this kind of learning is that it is automatic.

When you first started to learn Chinese, the characters look complicated and confusing. This book helps you to develop, through visual learning, the ability to extract critical information —structure, patterns and relationships between strokes—from Chinese characters so you will develop the perceptual skills to discern such information on your own. Switch off your other modes (listening, writing, speaking) of learning and focus just on seeing for the time being.

What is Novel in this Book

1. Applying Geometry to Chinese

Despite the capability to 'see', natives have trouble describing how they manage to recognise and differentiate so many characters instantaneously. Not all perceptual skills lend themselves to verbal description. Hence, it was a challenge to describe the perceptual skills required to decipher Chinese characters. This book boldly applied concepts used in an unrelated field— geometry to introduce new terminologies to describe features of characters.

Similar to constructing a building, Chinese characters are created with balance, symmetry and coordination between different components in mind. A stroke is tilted at a particular angle, fitted into a precise position and adjusted to different lengths with the aim to create a masterpiece. Geometrical jargons are perfect descriptors of these unnamed features. Such a connection between two unrelated subjects is an unconventional and groundbreaking way to view Chinese characters in new light.

2. What-You-See-Is-What-You-Name: 35 Basic Strokes

This book fills the missing gap that other books hardly paid attention to. It focuses on the most basic component—strokes. Skipping this fundamental learning is like learning English vocabularies without learning how to write the alphabets. It is easy to figure out the 26 English alphabets on your own but this is not the case for Chinese characters ... only 35 basic strokes but there are a myraid of possible combinations of these strokes.

In this book, the 35 strokes are given names that describe their appearances ... **what you see is what you name**! For instance, '7-Bend' looks like the number '7' and 'L-Bend' looks like the alphabet 'L'. This is an improvement to the current way of naming these strokes, which can be confusing. They are named according to these features *vertical (shu)*, *horizontal (heng)*, *slashes (pie, na)*, *hook (gou, ti)*, *tick (ti)*, *dot (dian)*, *sharp bend (zhe)*, *round bend/curve (wan)* and a combination of these features. For instance, 'L7-Bends' is called '*shu zhe zhe*'; '7L-Bends' is called '*heng zhe zhe*' and 'Double-7 Hook' is called '*heng zhe zhe zhe gou*'.

3. Visual Learning

Usually Chinese characters are shown in black and have stick-like appearance. It is very difficult to look for differences in this kind of presentation. In this book, a lot of effort is spent on showcasing Chinese characters in a different light —supersizing them, using multi-colours, choosing fonts that show their 'shapely figures', highlighting prominent characteristics and extracting featured strokes ... This improved presentation makes differences and compositions of characters easily visible. To help you learn systematically and know where to focus on, the visual activities zoom in on specific features of Chinese characters one at a time.

4. Creative Problem Solving

Instead of receiving the knowledge passively, you will need to actively search for multiple ways to solve some of the activities. At the end of each learning session, you will be prompted with questions to help you reflect on what you have learnt.

For Those Who Prefer A Different Experience

If you have been struggling with Chinese, perhaps one of the reasons is that you are starting at too high a level ... learning characters ... you need to first learn the most basic component —strokes. This book provides an alternative way to learn Chinese characters! If writing by hand is a hurdle to your learning, reduce the time spent on it, skip this process and re-introduce it at a more appropriate stage ... but do not give up.

This book is designed for **anyone—with or without any knowledge of Chinese**. Beginners will build a strong foundation while intermediate and advanced learners will be enlightened by new perspectives gained from the book. Visual and kinesthetic learners will love this book as you will need to doodle, use geometric tools, colour, do paper-cutting, solve puzzles ...

For those who are used to reading alphabets arranged from left to right only, Chinese characters will open you up to see the world in a different way. For those who gave up learning Chinese halfway because you got more confused the more characters you learnt ... Restart here!

Simplified Chinese Characters

This book is created for those learning simplified Chinese characters, currently used in China, Singapore and countries that have introduced *HSK* (an international Chinese proficiency test administered by authorities in China). The whole series of books are created with application to a few thousands frequently-used simplified Chinese characters in mind.

See with Magic Lenses

This book will serve as an important **complement to other forms of curriculum and instruction**. You will enjoy learning Chinese more as you will be equipped with a pair of magic lenses to see Chinese characters differently.

This is the first book of a series of radically innovative books to guide you to learn Chinese characters systematically. It elicits the tacit knowledge that native speakers have internalised but have difficulty verbalising. You will benefit a lot from this book as such knowledge and skills require years of learning and honing.

It's Easy! It's Intuitive!

Look at these symbols. Make a good guess and match each of them to a suitable name based on their shapes.

● **Dot**   ● **7-Bend**   ● **Horizontal**   ● **Tick**

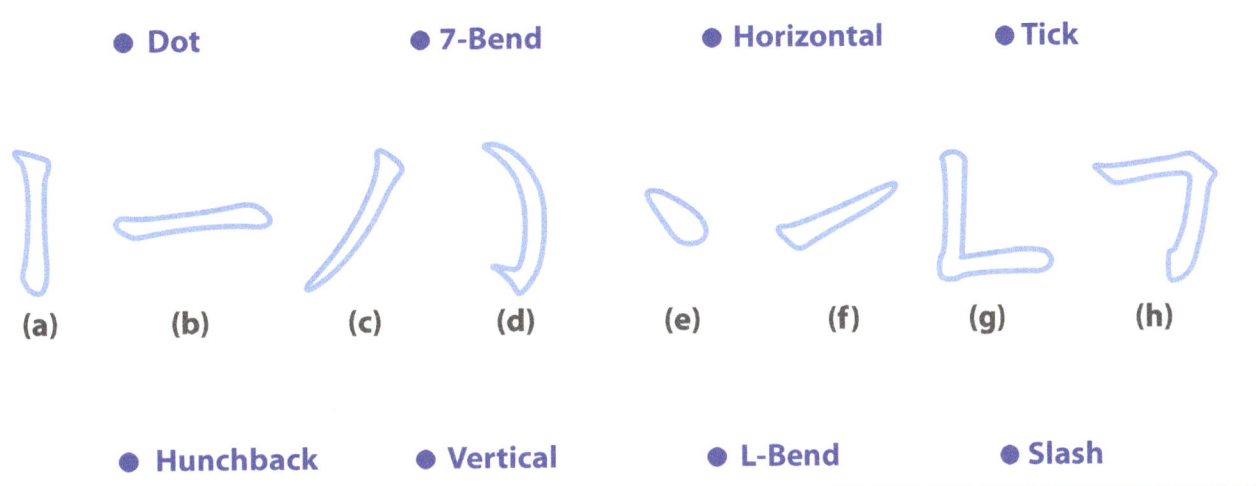

(a)   (b)   (c)   (d)   (e)   (f)   (g)   (h)

● **Hunchback**   ● **Vertical**   ● **L-Bend**   ● **Slash**

The next activity needs more brain cells. Match the stroke to a suitable name. Use your imagination. You can do it!

(a)   ●   **Boomerang**   ●   (d)

(b)   ●   **Lightning**   ●   (e)

●   **7L-Bends**   ●

(c)   ●   **L7-Bends**   ●   (f)

● **Double-7 Bends** ●

●   **Z-Hook**   ●

Complete the activities before checking the answers on page 2.

You'll love this book if you

Feel giddy looking at Chinese characters
They just look like a pile of entangling pickup sticks . . . you had a hard time figuring out which stick to pick out first.

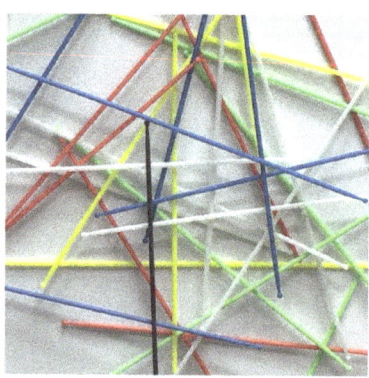

Have been confused by twinlike characters
which look almost identical.

Have been frustrated by unproductive writing drills
that are supposed to help you remember the characters.

Are a teacher
looking for creative activities to engage students in your lessons.

Want to get some sensing
before deciding whether to pick up the language.

You will need to

Interact with the Book
This is NOT a book to be read from start to end. There are plenty of activities to do and many of them could be done in more than one way. Explore the possibilties using your creativity!

Use Different Tools
Use any tool that can help you complete the activities. Here are some of the tools that you can consider using. Have fun!

Basic Geometry
Before starting, revise these geometry concepts that will be applied to analyse Chinese characters.

1. Angles

a) Right angle

90°

b) Acute angle

> 0°
< 90°

2. Slopes

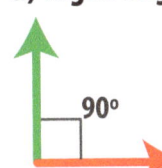

a) Positive gradient

b) Negative gradient

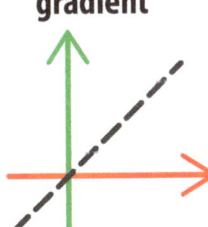

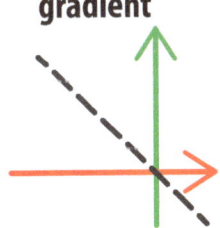

Find out more about geometry in Section 4

This book is about . . .

① Chinese Characters

Learn the most basic component—strokes

How these strokes combine

How they form beautiful characters

③ Creative Problem Solving

Use more than one method to solve the problems.

② Geometry

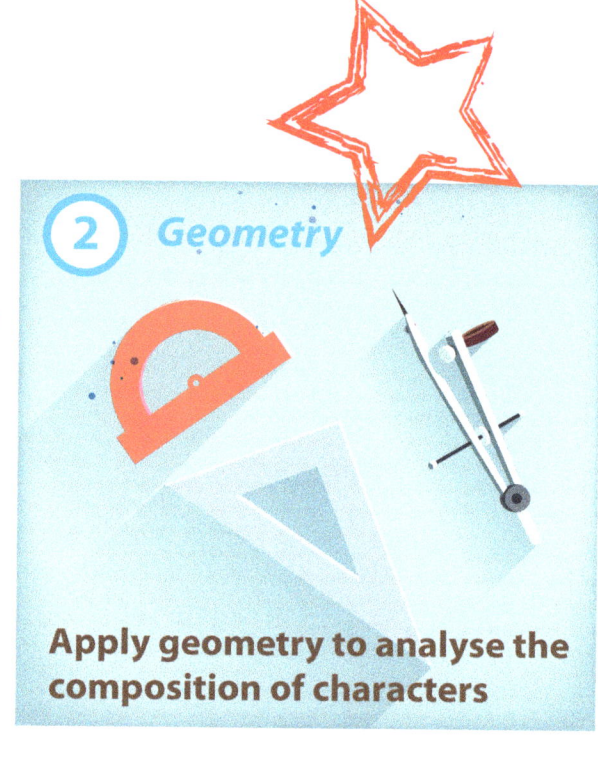

Apply geometry to analyse the composition of characters

Depending on your interests and motivation, you may focus on a different area. A total beginner may focus on learning the strokes while an intermediate learner may want to take up the challenge to solve the problems in different ways. This is a book that you can keep rereading and redoing the activities to gain a deeper understanding.

Content

List of Activities

Introduction

3

Adapt
Balance
Centre

2

Apart
Bonding
Crossing

1

Angles
Bends
Curves

Triple
ABCs
Concept

What-You-See-Is-What-You-Name

Check answers here.

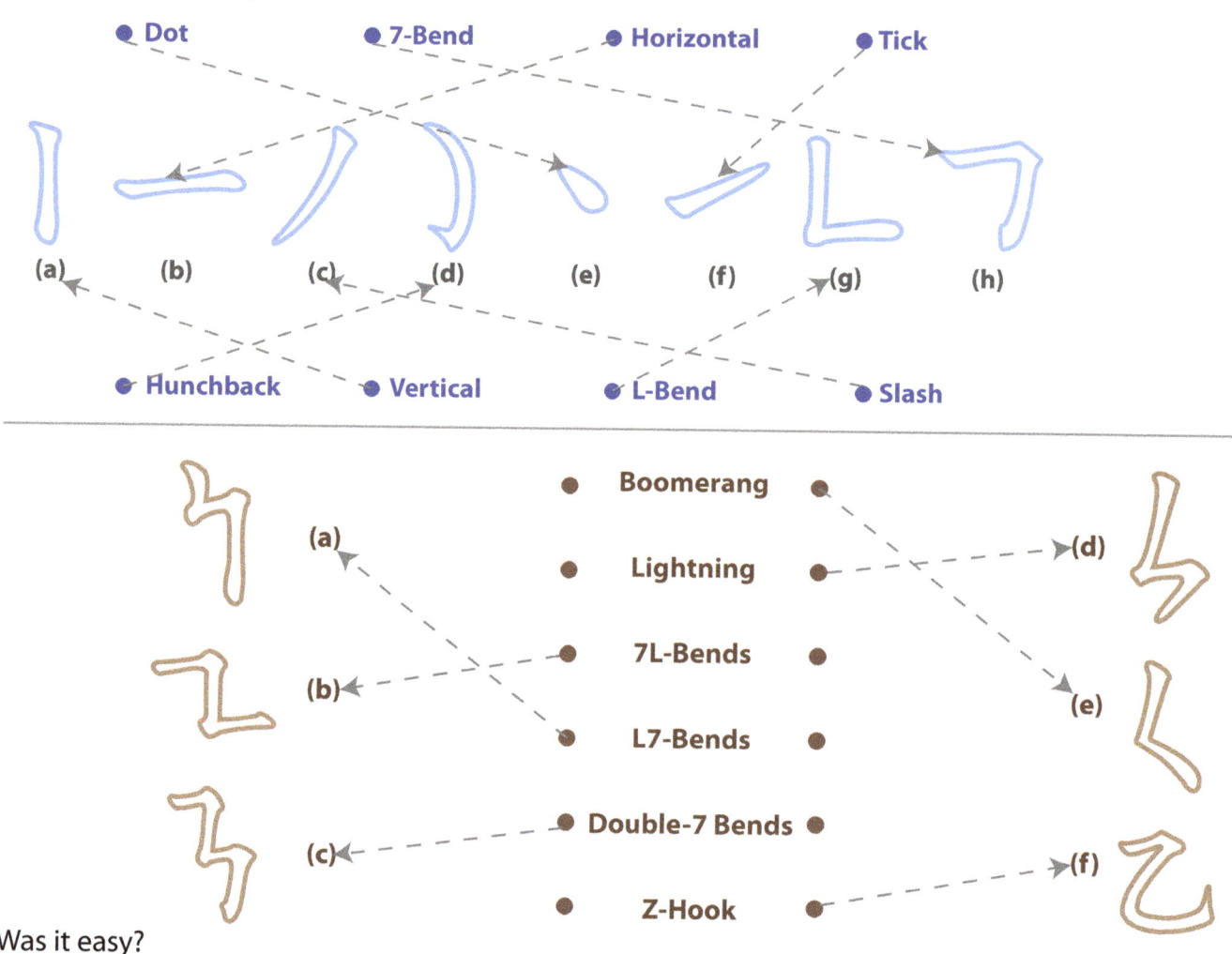

Was it easy?

We name the strokes according to what you see. A vertical is called a vertical, a horizontal a horizontal and so on. It's intuitive!

If you are still curious what are the Chinese names of these strokes, check out in Section 4.

Is it Necessary to Learn Chinese Characters?

I just want to learn to speak Mandarin, can I just learn the Romanized phonetics (Hanyu pinyin) and skip learning the characters?

Can You Believe it?

The same Hanyu pinyin 'spelling' (shishi) can yield more than 30 different vocabularies with the same pronunciation*. So, it is easy to begin with Hanyu pinyin, but you will be on an uphill climb ... because the more vocabularies you learn, the more confused you will get.

湿湿　试试　十世　世世　石狮　实实　诗史　事事　视事　史诗　石室　矢石　适时　时时　失势　试室　shishi　施事　实时　事实　失事　世事　失时　时势　实施　失实　是是　失恃　史实　师事　实事　誓师　时世　逝世　时事

These vocabularies are pronounced as 'shishi' but in different tones.

4　INTRODUCTION

Is it Necessary to Learn to Write by Hand?

Is it necessary to learn to write Chinese characters by hand? Many teachers and learners think it is a good way to remember the stroke order and to distinguish between similar-looking Chinese characters. Research also suggested that studying Chinese and learning to write Chinese characters may train a whole array of cognitive abilities not developed by studying other writing systems.

However, the reality is many learners dread writing practices and are unable to appreciate its benefits. One possible reason could be writing exercises in textbooks often lack meaningful purposes. So, learners find that they are doing a mundane task ... copying the characters stroke by stroke. They probably could remember these characters better than those that they have not written but it is certainly not the most productive use of time, and probably not the most enjoyable activity for some learners. To make the matter worse, many young learners are so burdened by it that they resorted to 'drawing' these characters like any other patterns they come across in art classes, without an in-depth understanding of their stroke sequence, composition ...

Perhaps we should **start learning Chinese with NO writing**! Like in art classes, before you start to draw you have to observe the lines, curves, shapes ... of the objects you are going to draw and learn to appreciate beautiful art creations. You play with colours, dabble in playful colouring ... only then are you ready to draw and paint seriously. Similarly, in Chinese lessons the first task is not to write or to read (for meaning) but just analyse the composition of these characters ... observe their curvy figures, solid bends, cute dots ... see how they combine and interact with one another to form beautiful characters. What is missing in Chinese lessons is explaining to learners the intricate composition of characters and showing them how to appreciate Chinese characters like art.

In this book *Learn Chinese WITHOUT Writing (LCWW)*, we are advocating other ways to learn Chinese characters. Characters can be analysed visually and explained using geometry concepts (e.g. angles, arcs, shapes). Instead of giving repetitive handwriting practices of the same characters, we introduce activities that engage learners' other senses. These activities could be colouring, drawing, solving puzzles, using different tools or art and craft. More importantly, learners will be encouraged to do the activities in multiple ways and devise their own ways of remembering the ideas learnt. If you really hate writing (or are unable to write), just find your own way to learn the concepts taught in that activity and skip the writing part.

Triple **ABC**s Concept

KEY SECTIONS

THE STORY

Section 1:

FEATURES OF STROKES

Angles

Bends

Curves

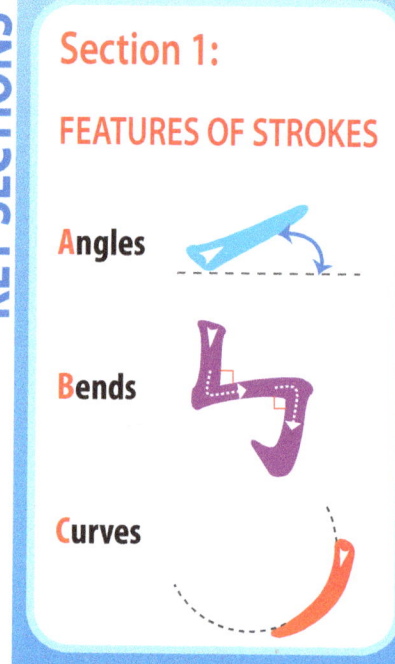

Section 2:

WAYS OF COMBINING THE STROKES

Apart

Bonding

Crossing

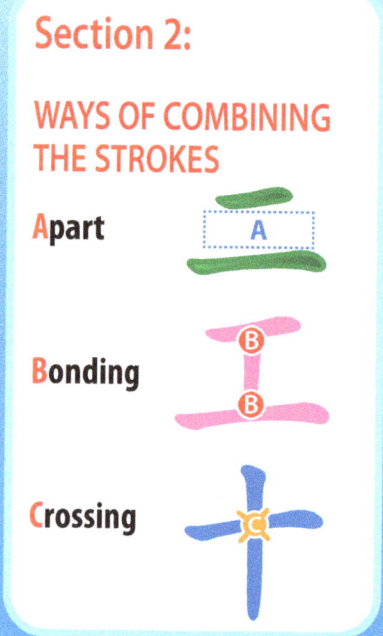

Section 3:

UNSPOKEN RULESOF CHINESE CHARACTERS

Adapt

Balance

Centre

PERFORMERS

Performing Teams: 8

Number of Members: 35
1. Straight (5 members, 1 Team)
2. Curve (5 members, 1 Team)
3. Dot (3 members, 1 Team)
4. Bend (22 members, 5 Teams)

FORMATIONS

Working with one another:

Performers have to learn to work with members from any teams. When performing, they have to stay **a**part, **b**ond with or **c**ross (intersect) another performer to create formations.

PERFORMANCE TECHNIQUES

Performing on Box Stage:

Performers have to be able to **a**dapt to fit into the box stage so that the formation produced will look **b**alanced and **c**entred.

> **Terms used in the Story**
> 1. Strokes = Performers
> 2. Characters = Formations
> 3. Square Box = Box Stage

6   **INTRODUCTION**

Use Your Imagination

Before we can understand how Chinese characters work, we need to expand our imagination on 'strokes', the most basic component of Chinese characters. We need to enter their world . . .

Performers

Imagine strokes as performers and their job is to work as a team to create a beautiful piece of art—a Chinese character—within the limited space of a box stage. Each stroke has its unique characteristics and vie for your attention to notice its talents.

How will the strokes work with one another? To put up a good performance, they need to meet some requirements such as being able to work in teams, knowing the limitations and requirements of a stage. If we can understand the behind-the-scenes secrets of churning out good 'performances', we will be able to write Chinese characters correctly and beautifully. This ability to recognise and distinguish characters will form the groundwork for your next stage of learning.

Triple ABCs Concept

The life and work of strokes can be explained using the 'Triple ABCs Concept' which consists of three sets of ABC:

1. **Angles, Bends, Curves**
2. **Apart, Bonding, Crossing**
3. **Adapt, Balance, Centre**

The first set of ABC explains the characteristics of strokes; the second set is on how the strokes combine with one another to create characters and the last set reveals the aesthetic requirements of characters.

The Story

To many people, strokes are like tadpoles

Actually, they are ...

Colourful Performers

with unique talents

on a journey ...

to work together with other performers

APART
BOND
CROSS

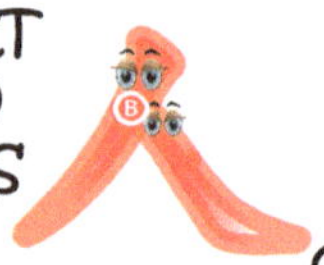

to create FORMATIONS

The challenge is to do so within a BOX STAGE

and learn to ADAPT,

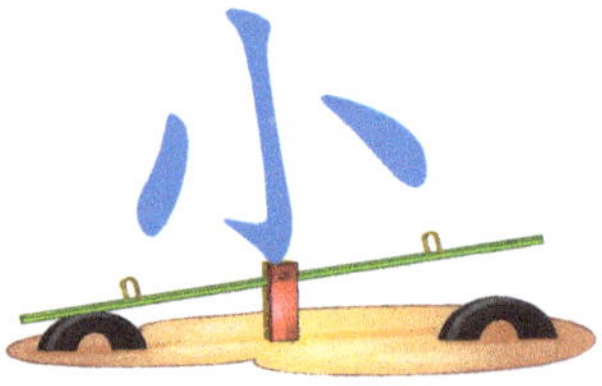

BALANCE and

CENTRE themselves within the box

so as to create a beautiful formation !

3
Adapt
Balance
Centre

2
Apart
Bonding
Crossing

1
Angles
Bends
Curves

Triple
ABCs
Concept

Angles

a) Angle to the Horizontal

Describes the slope of a stroke by measuring the angle it makes with the horizontal.

b) Angle of Bends

Describes the angle made by different types of bends

Bends

a) 7-Bend

b) L-Bend

c) Combinations of Bends

Curves

a) Slash

b) Curl

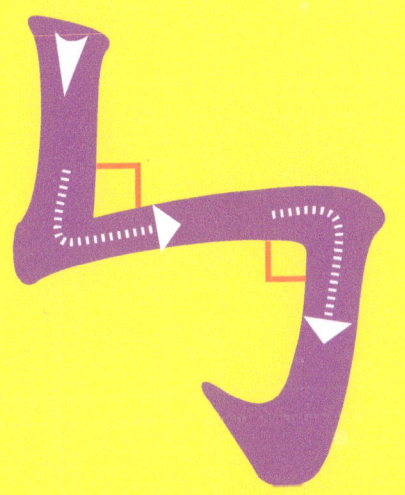

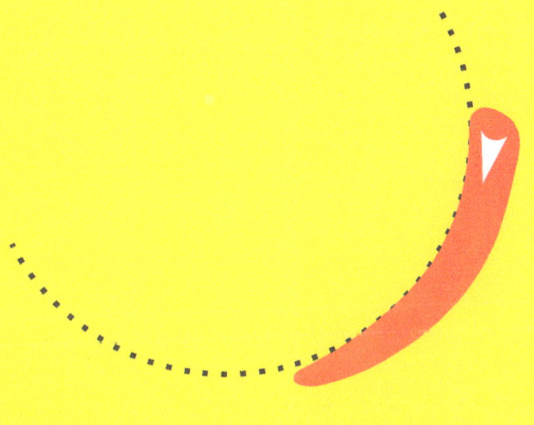

Performers

The first set of ABC (Angles, Bends and Curves) describes the characteristics of the 35 strokes (performers) that make up Chinese characters (formations).

1.
Four Representatives

2.
Eight Families

3.
35 Performers

Four Representatives of Performers

There are 35 Performers ... before we meet them let's meet the representative of each family... their nicknames are Mr Straight, Miss Curve, Baby Dot and Mr 7-Bend.

Mr Straight

Miss Curve

Baby Dot

Mr 7-Bend

Observe them carefully. Each of them is unique. Mr Straight stands absolutely straight like a soldier; Miss Curve likes to curve her body like a dancer; Baby Dot is small compared to others and Mr 7-Bend looks strong, maintaining his posture with a right-angle (90º) bend .

Eight Families

Mr Straight, Miss Curve and Baby Dot each has a family while Mr 7-Bend represents five families.

+ **One bend:** Mr 7-Bend and Mr-LBend
+ **More than one bend:** Mr L7-Bends, Mr 7L-Bends and Mr Double-7 Bends

Characteristics of Each Family

1. Mr Straight

All the members in Mr Straight's family have straight bodies.

Vertical

Vertical stands upright at 90° to the ground.

Horizontal

Horizontal can do planking, that is keep its body horizontal.

2. Miss Curve

All the members in Miss Curve's family have curvy figures.

Slash

Slash slants its body at an angle to the horizontal and tapers off at its end.

Hunchback (Curl)

Curl curls its back like an arc and has a hook attached to its end.

3. Baby Dot

All the members in Baby Dot's family are small and cute.

Dot

Dot slants its body downwards.

Tick

Tick tilts its body upwards and tapers off at its end.

4. Mr 7-Bend

All the members in Mr 7-Bend's family bow forward like number 7.

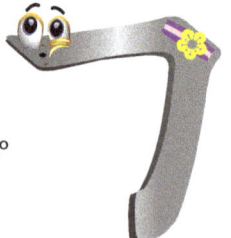

7-Bend

7-Bend bows forward at 90° (right angle).

Acute-7

Acute-7 bows forward at less than 90° (acute angle).

5. Mr L-Bend

All the members in Mr L-Bend's family have one bend

L-Bend

L-Bend has a 90° bend and sits like the alphabet L.

Acute-L

Acute-L has an acute-angle bend.

6. Mr L7-Bends

All the members in Mr L7-Bends' family have two bends and start with L-Bend or Acute-L

L7-Bends

L7-Bends has two 90° bends.

Lightning (Acute-L7)

Lightning has two acute bends.

7. Mr 7L-Bends

All the members in Mr 7L-Bends' family have two bends and a flat base, and start with 7-Bend or Acute-7.

7L-Bends

7L-Bends has two 90° bends.

Z-Hook

Z-Hook has a hook, two acute-angle bends and one of the bends is round.

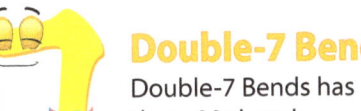

Double-7 Bends

Double-7 Bends has three 90° bends.

Acute-7 Hunchback

Acute-7 Hunchback starts with Acute-7 and ends with Hunchback.

8. Mr Double-7 Bends

All the members in Mr Double-7 Bends' family are formed by 7-Bend or Acute-7 combined with another stroke.

Meet Mr Straight's Family

(A) Verticals

All verticals stand upright at 90° to the ground

<table>
<tr><td>

1. Mr Straight's Family

Number of members: 5
Characteristics: Straight lines
Types: Vertical and Horizontal

</td></tr>
</table>

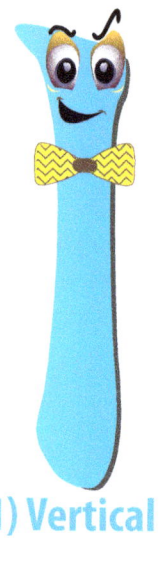

1) Vertical

2) Vertical Left Hook
With a left hook

3) Vertical Right Hook
With a right hook

(B) Horizontals

All horizontals lie almost parallel (0°) to the ground

4) Horizontal

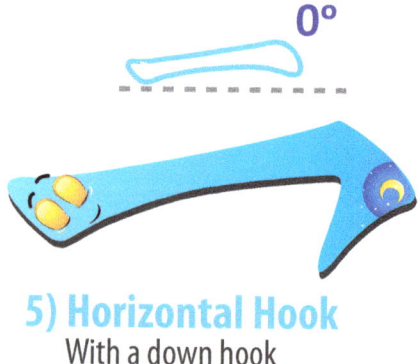

0°

5) Horizontal Hook
With a down hook

18   ANGLES, BENDS & CURVES

Activity 1
Straight Lines with Hook

Highlight *Vertical Left Hook* in these characters:

Highlight *Horizontal Hook* in these characters:

Highlight *Vertical Right Hook* in these characters:

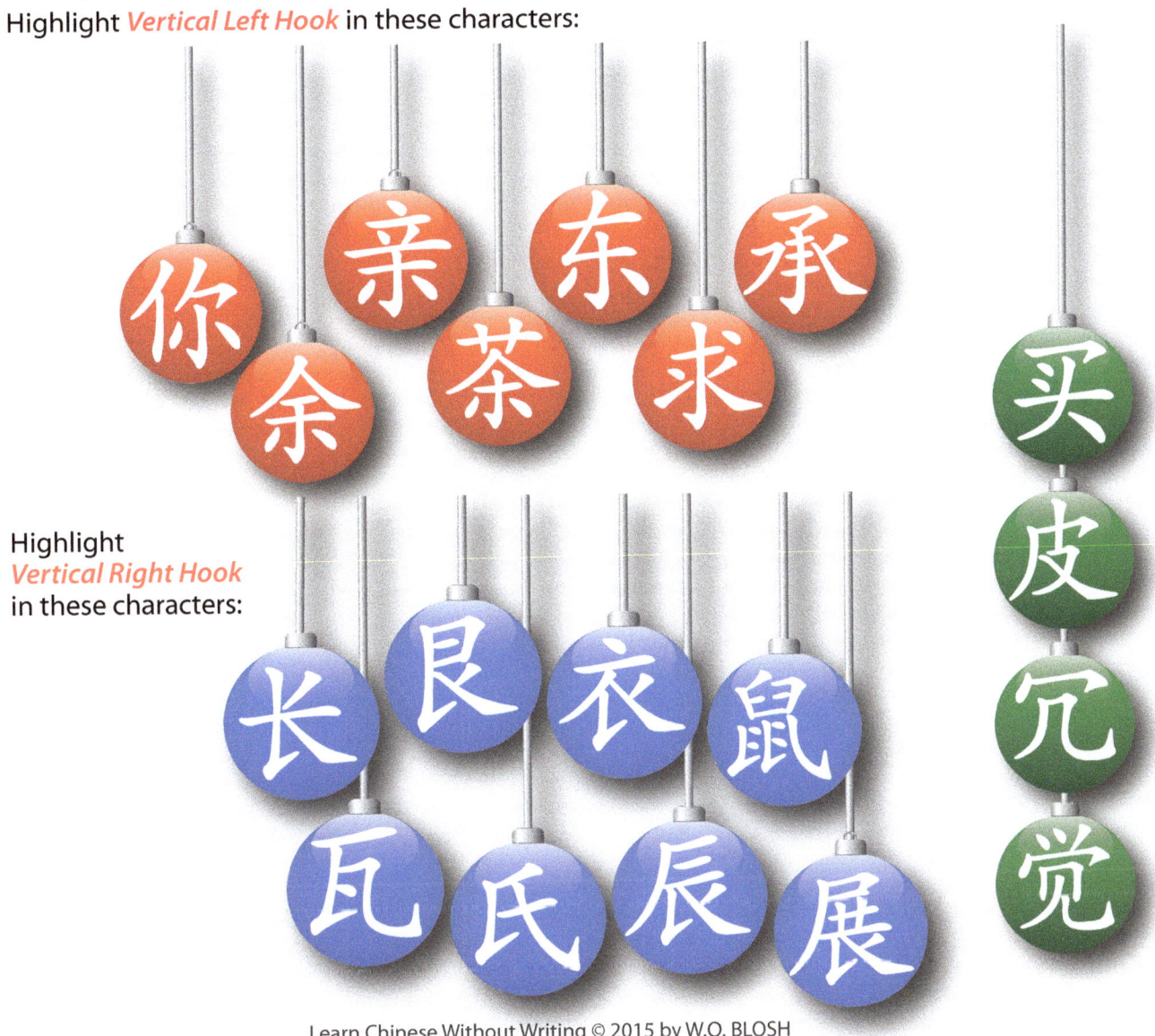

Learn Chinese Without Writing © 2015 by W.Q. BLOSH

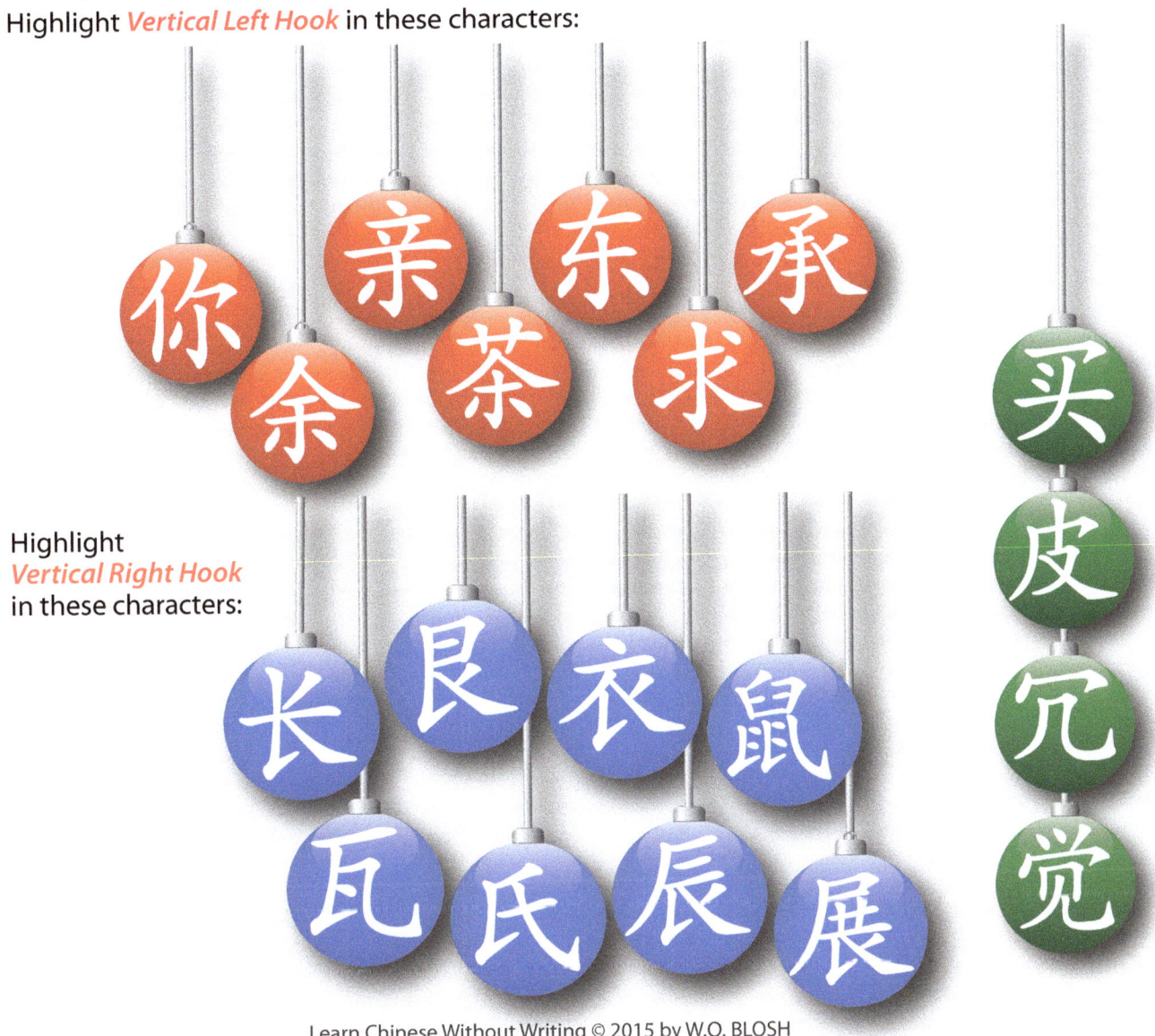

Straight Lines with Hook

1. How does each stroke appear in different characters? (e.g. Longer? Shorter?)
2. Is that stroke isolated or does it interact with other strokes?
3. What kind of interactions these strokes have with other strokes?
   (e.g. Touches? Cuts across?)

Write down your own questions.
Feel free to describe and illustrate
in your own way.

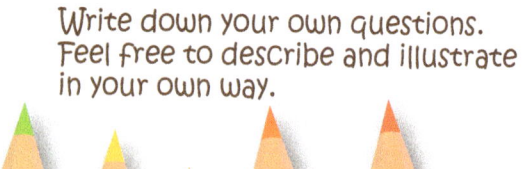

My Questions:

My Imagination of the Strokes

Use your imagination, what do the **five members in Mr Straight's Family** remind you of?

Create your own sketchbook!
Add clippings. Doodle, Make Notes,
Summarise . . .

Meet Miss Curve's Family

2. Miss Curve's Family
Number of members: 5
Characteristics: Curvy figures
Types: Slash and Curl

(A) Slashes

Slashes slant at an angle (less than 90º) to the horizontal and tapers off at the end.

1. RL-Slash

Slants downwards from **right to left** and has a positive slope.

2. LR-Slash

Slants downwards from **left to right** and has a negative slope.

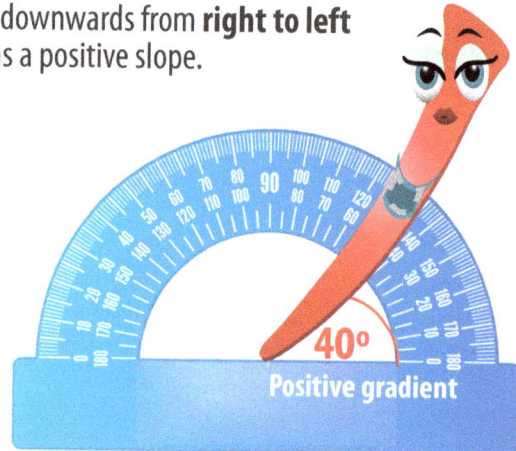

40º
Positive gradient

55º
Negative gradient

(B) Curls

All curls curl up their body at an angle to the horizontal and has a hook

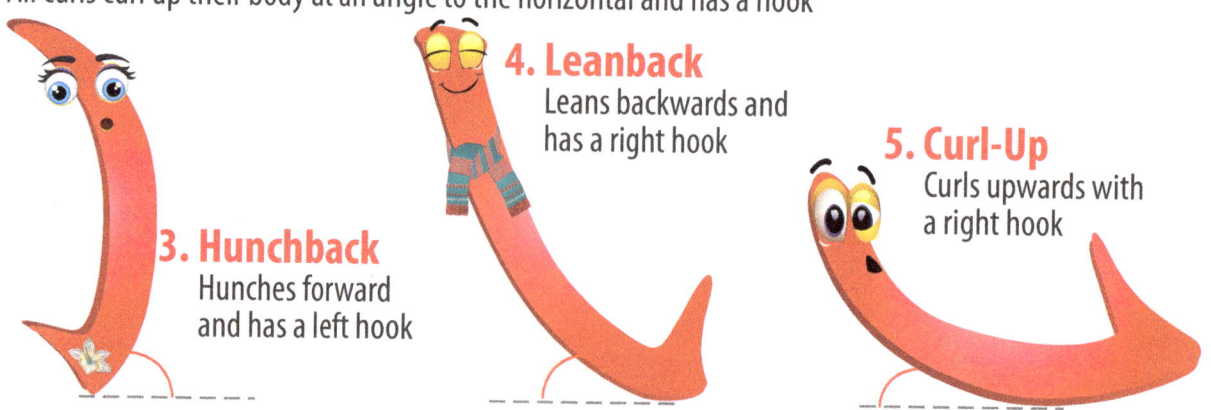

4. Leanback
Leans backwards and has a right hook

5. Curl-Up
Curls upwards with a right hook

3. Hunchback
Hunches forward and has a left hook

Activity 2
RL-Slash

The RL-Slashes of these characters are extracted. RL-slashes slant at different angles to the horizontal when they appear in different characters.

Identify where the highlighted RL-Slash comes from. Draw a line to match the character to the RL-Slash lined up here. See examples.

Use any tool to do this activity. Explore as many ways of solving as you can.

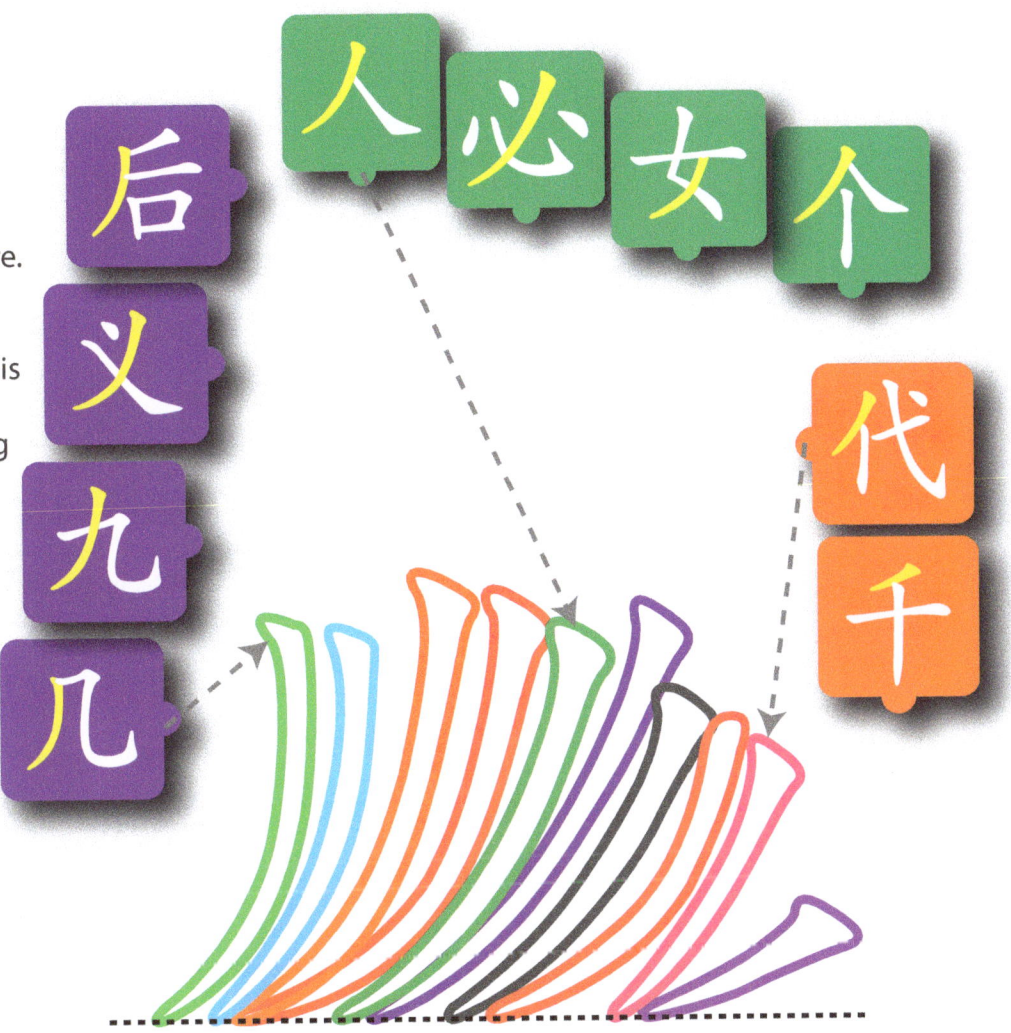

Learn Chinese Without Writing © 2015 by W.Q. BLOSH

Activity 3
LR-Slash

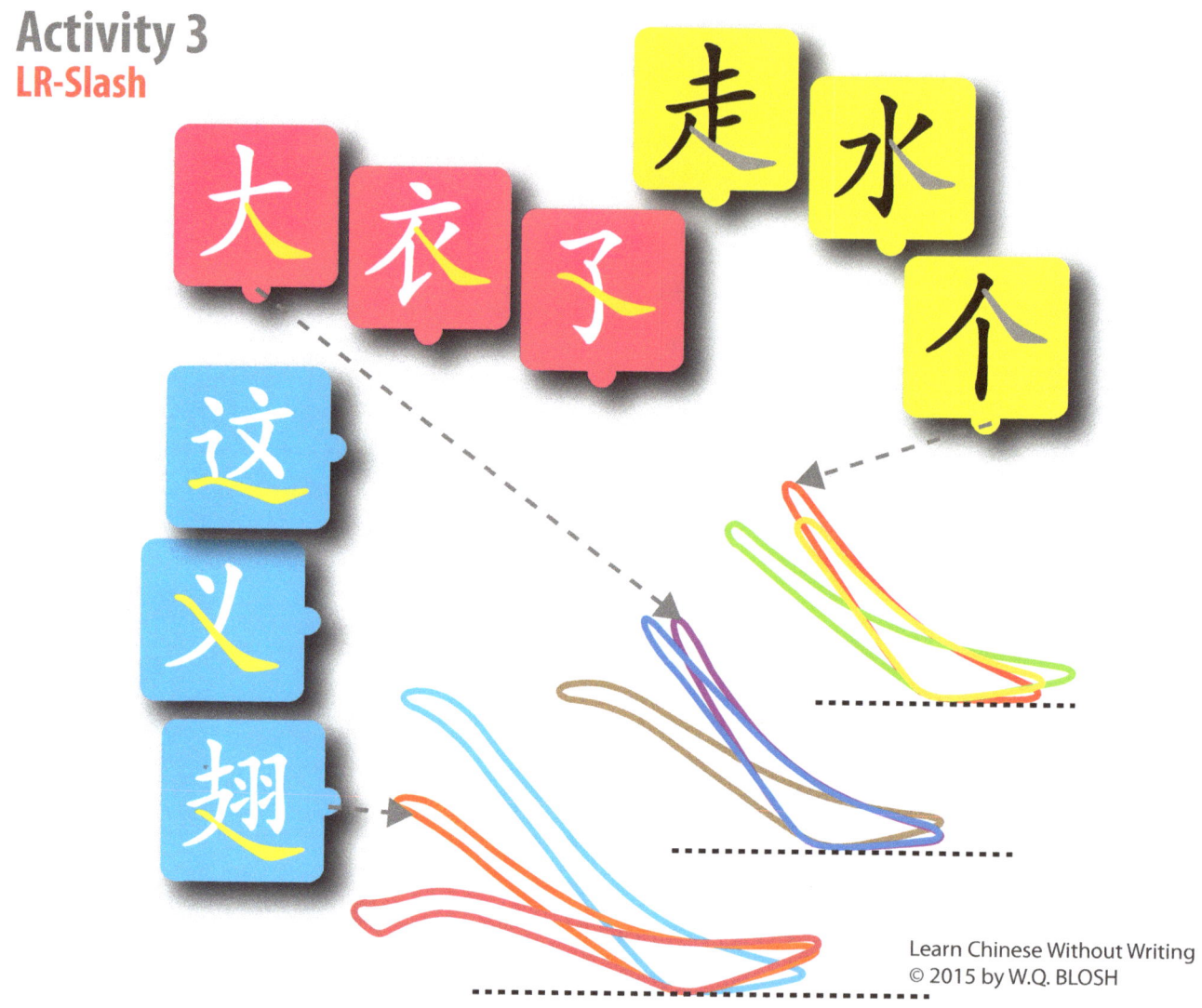

Learn Chinese Without Writing
© 2015 by W.Q. BLOSH

Like RL-Slash, LR-Slashes from different characters also slant at different angles to the horizontal. The only difference is they are slanting in the opposite direction.

Use a different method from the previous activity to do this activity. If you only used your naked eyes for the previous activity, try to use a tool in this activity. Identify where the LR-Slash comes from. Draw a line to match the character to the LR-Slash. See examples.

Activity 4
Curls

Identify where the Curls come from. Draw a line to match the character to the curl. See example. Use your creativity, think of another way to solve this problem.

Learn Chinese Without Writing
© 2015 by W.Q. BLOSH

RL-Slashes, LR-Slashes and Curls

1. Which part of a stroke (e.g. head? tail? middle? body?) touches or intersects with another stroke?
2. Do these strokes have positive or negative gradient (slope)?
3. Which is the steepest stroke? Which is the gentlest slope?
4. What is the <u>angle to the horizontal</u> made by each stroke? (use any tool)
5. For Curls, how does the <u>size of the circle</u> relate to the <u>curviness of the stroke</u>? (e.g. smaller circle, less curvy)

My Reflection

Write down your own questions. Feel free to describe and illustrate in your own way.

My Questions:

My Imagination of the Strokes

Use your imagination, what do the **five members in Miss Curve's Family** remind you of?

Create your own sketchbook! Add clippings. Doodle, Make Notes, Summarise . . .

Meet Baby Dot's Family

3. Baby Dot's Family
Number of members: 3
Characteristics: Small
Types: Dot and Tick

(A) Dots

All dots are short, tilt at an angle to the
horizontal and slant **downwards**

Positive gradient

Negative gradient

1. RL-Dot
Slants downwards from **right to left**

2. LR-Dot
Slants downwards from **left to right**

(B) Tick

The tick is longer than dot and tilts **upwards** at an angle to the horizontal

3. Tick
Points upwards
from **left to right**

Activity 5
Dots and Tick

Colour these strokes
using these colours:
1) RL-Dot: Red
2) LR-Dot: Green
3) Tick: Blue

See example.

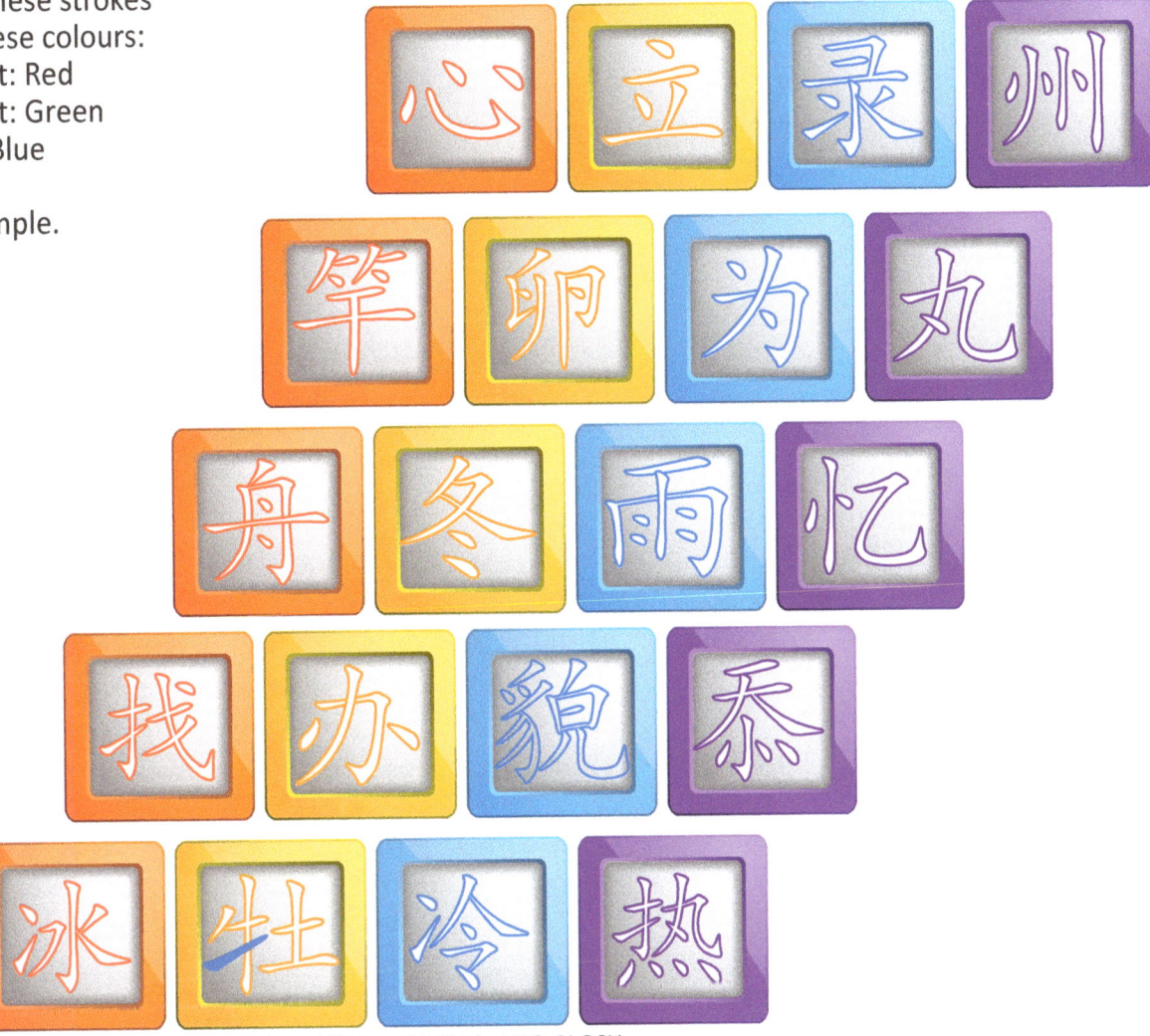

Dots and Tick

1. How frequently do RL-Dot, LR-Dot and Tick appear in the characters? Which stroke has the highest frequency of appearance?
2. When the **dots and tick** appear side by side, how many ways are there to position them? Feel free to draw to show.
3. Where on the character does a Tick usually appear? (e.g. Left? Right?)
4. Which part of a stroke (e.g. head? tail? middle? body?) touches or intersects with another stroke?
5. Do these strokes have positive or negative gradient?

My Reflection

Write down your own questions.
Feel free to describe and illustrate in your own way.

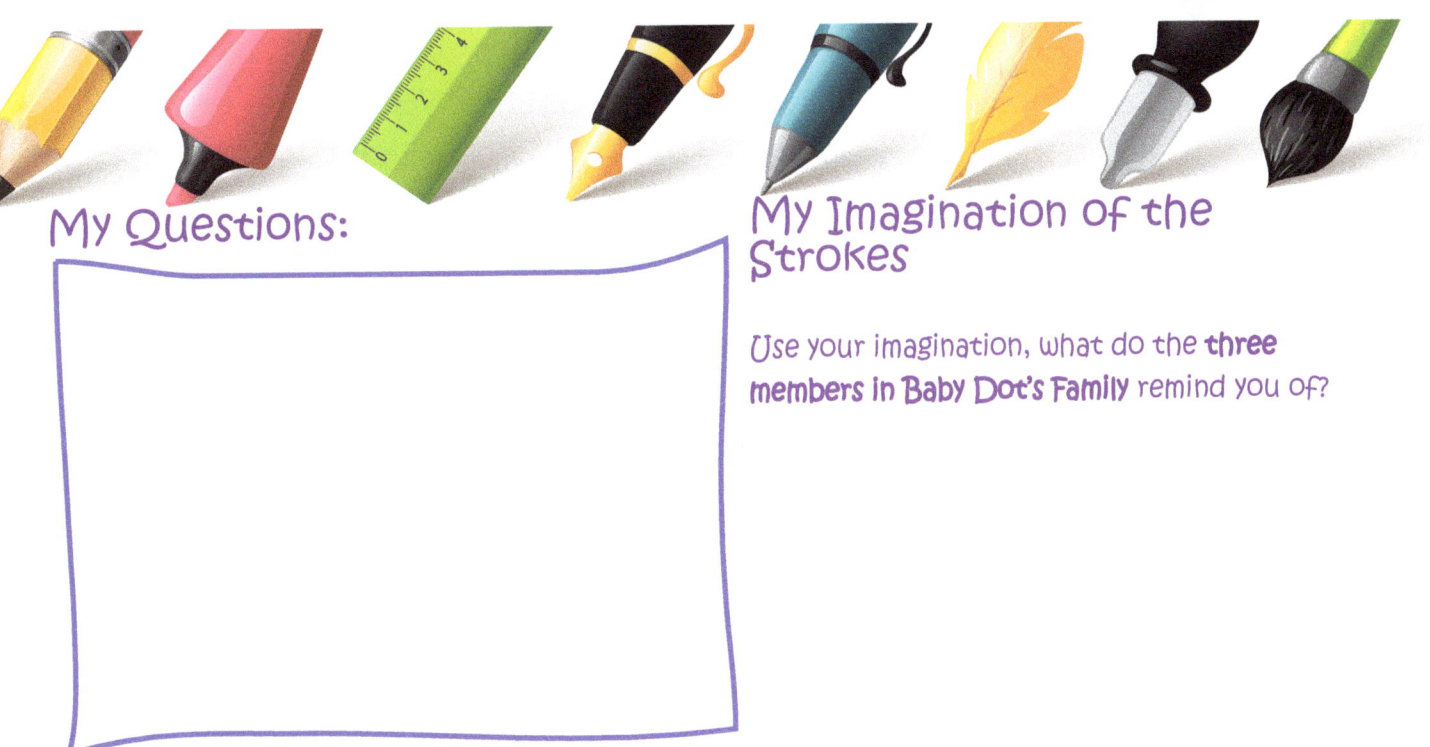

My Questions:

My Imagination of the Strokes

Use your imagination, what do the **three members in Baby Dot's Family** remind you of?

Create your own sketchbook! Add clippings.
Doodle, Make Notes, Summarise . . .

What You've Learnt

Angle to the Horizontal

The slope/gradient of a stroke is measured by the angle it makes with the horizontal.

❖ A vertically upright stroke is 90° to the horizontal while a horizontal stroke is 0° to the horizontal.

❖ Dots, tick, slashes and curls all inclined at an angle to the horizontal.

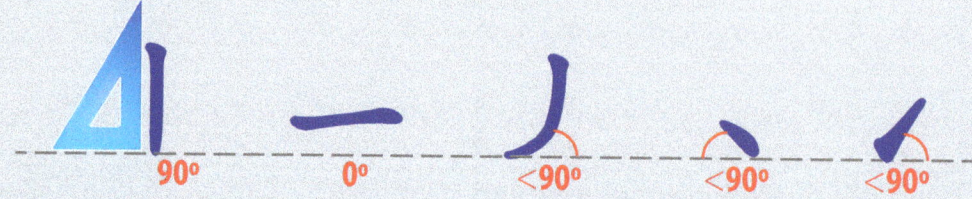

'Slashes' versus 'Curls'

Similarities

❖ They are both curvy.

❖ Their curves are the arcs of circles of different sizes.

❖ They slant at different angles to the horizontal.

Differences

❖ The three Curls, Hunchback, Leanback and Curl-up, all have a hook attached to them.

❖ For Slashes, their ends taper off—becoming narrower and thinner.

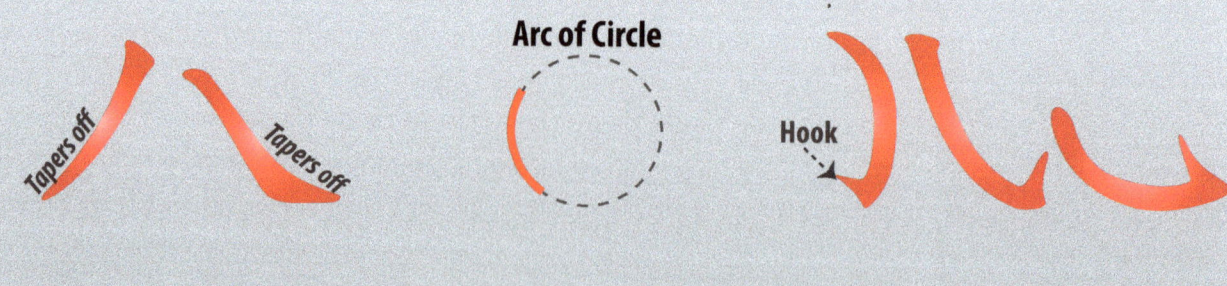

'Hook' versus 'Tick'

Similarities

❖ Both start at the bottom and move upwards, tapering off at the end.

Differences

❖ A Hook is attached to another stroke (e.g. Vertical, Horizontal, Curl) and becomes part of the stroke. When a Hook is attached to a Vertical on its left side, it becomes 'Vertical Left Hook'.

❖ A Tick can be apart from other strokes or it can intersects with another stroke.

a) Apart

Hook

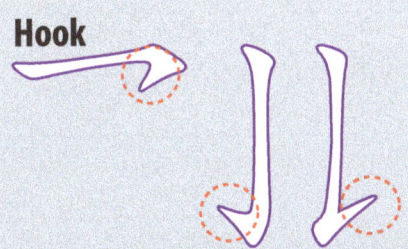

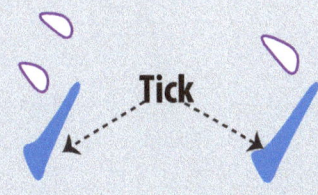

Tick

b) Intersect Another Stroke

Tick intersects with another stroke

Hook facing left

4. Mr 7-Bend's Family

Number of members: **6**
Characteristics: **7-Shape**
Types: **7-Bend and Acute-7**

Meet Mr 7-Bend's Family

(A) 7-Bend

Bends forward like number 7 at about 90º (right angle)

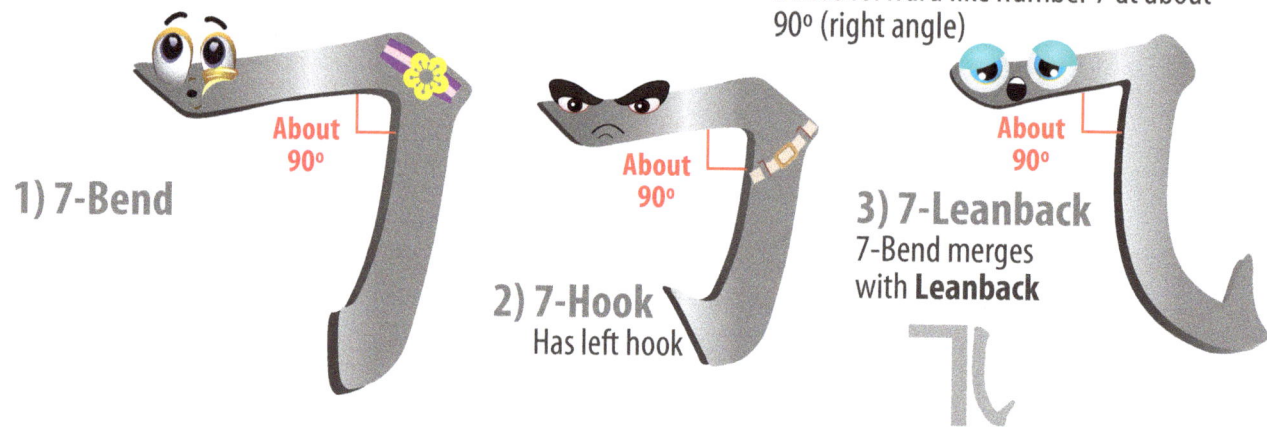

1) 7-Bend

About 90º

2) **7-Hook**
Has left hook

About 90º

3) 7-Leanback
7-Bend merges with **Leanback**

About 90º

(B) Acute-7

Bends forward like number 7 at less than 90º (acute angle)

4) **Acute-7**
Bends at acute angle

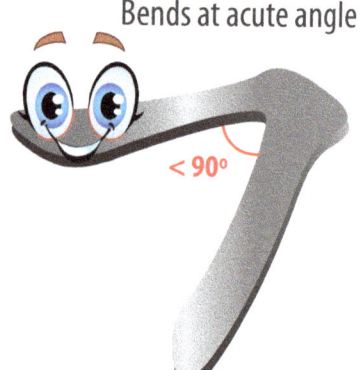

< 90º

5) **7-Slash**
Acute-7 merges with **RL-Slash**

< 90º

6) 7-Back kick
Acute-7 merges with **Vertical Right Hook.**
It looks like someone kicking backwards

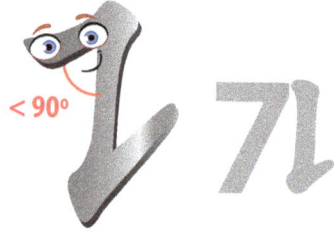

< 90º

Activity 6
7-Bend, 7-Hook and Acute-7

The width and height of 7-Bend vary for different characters. Identify where the 7-Bend or 7-Hook comes from. Write the alphabet in the bracket.
(Clues: Measure the relative length of the horizontal part and the vertical part. Take a close look at the angle of bend of each stroke.)

7-Bend, 7-Hook and Acute-7

1. Observe how each stroke appears in different characters? What are the <u>relative lengths</u> of the horizontal and vertical parts?

2. What is the <u>angle of bend</u> in each stroke? Which has the biggest angle? Which has the smallest angle?

3. What are the stroke(s) (if any) surrounded by 7-Hook?

My Reflection

Write down your own questions. Feel free to describe and illustrate in your own way.

My Questions:

My Imagination of the Strokes

Use your imagination, what do the **six members in Mr 7-Bend's** Family remind you of?

Create your own sketchbook! Add clippings. Doodle, Make Notes, Summarise . . .

Meet Mr L-Bend's Family

(A) L-Bend

All the L-Bends have right-angle bend and sit like the capital letter L

5. Mr L-Bend's Family
Number of members: 5
Characteristics: Variations of L-Shape
Types: L-Bend and Acute-L

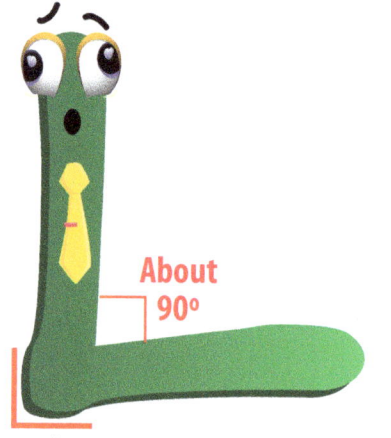

About 90°

1) L-Bend
With a sharp bend

About 90°

2) Round-L
With a round bend

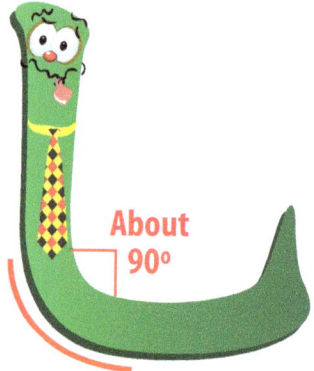

About 90°

3) L-Hook
With a round bend and right hook

30° clockwise

About 90°

4) Boomerang
Has a sharp bend, rotates about 30° clockwise and looks like a boomerang

(B) Acute-L
The angle of bend is less than 90° (acute angle)

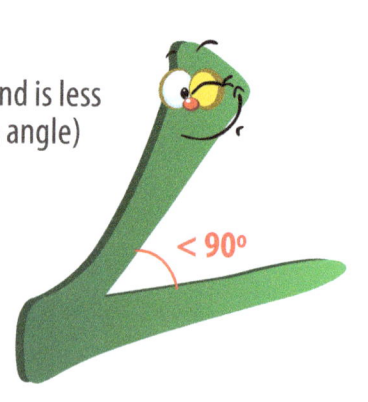

5) Acute-L

< 90°

Activity 7

L-Bend Family

Now, you should be good at this kind of activities. This activity is relatively easy compared to the previous ones. Identify where the L-Bend, L-Hook, Boomerang and Acute-L come from. Write the alphabet in the bracket.

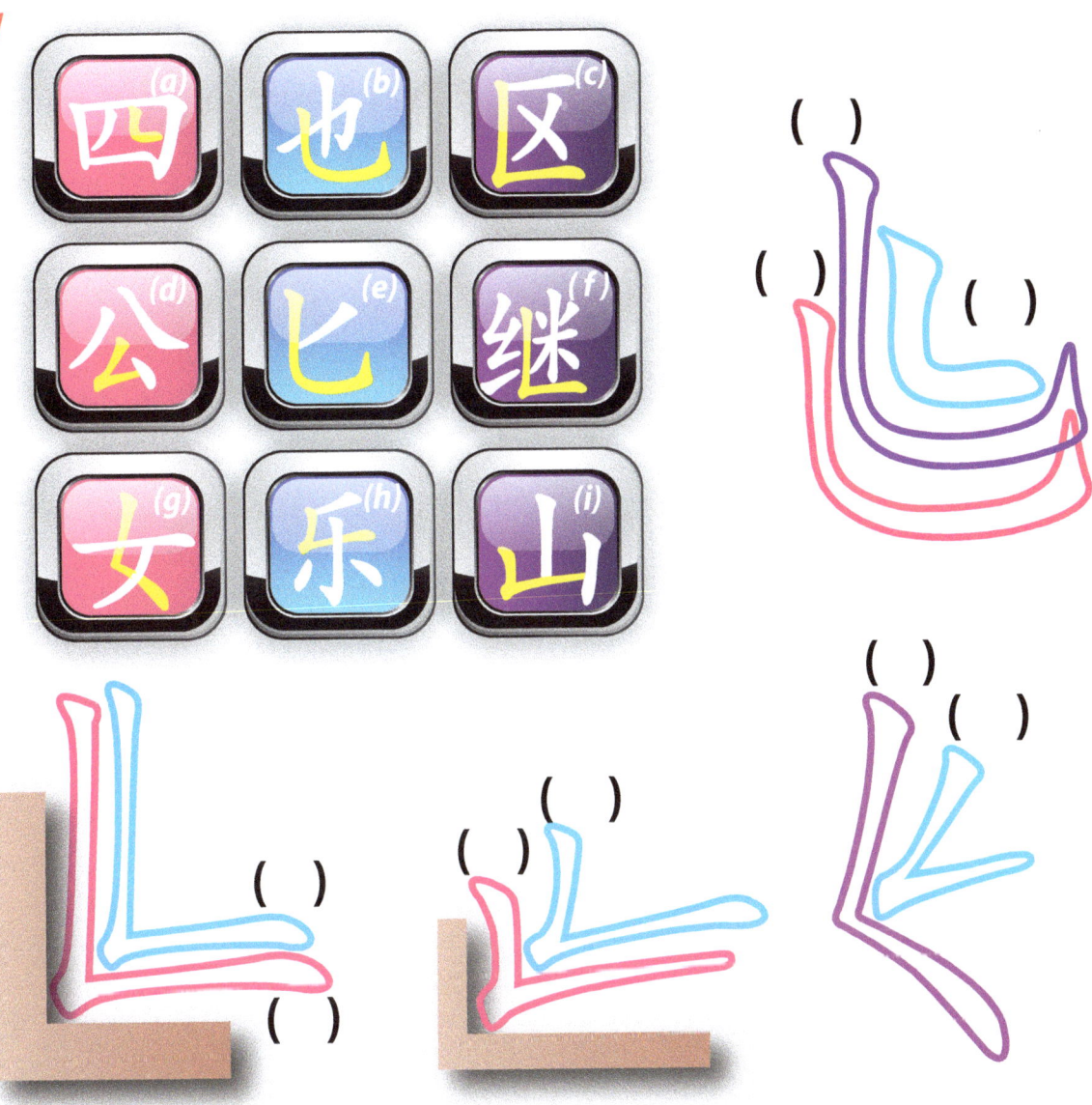

四 (a)　也 (b)　区 (c)
公 (d)　乚 (e)　继 (f)
女 (g)　乐 (h)　山 (i)

( )　( )　( )
( )　( )
( )　( )　( )
( )

L-Bend Family

1. Observe how the stroke appears in different characters? What are the <u>relative lengths</u> of the horizontal and vertical parts? Which is longer—the horizontal or vertical part?
2. What is the <u>angle of bend</u> in each stroke?
3. What stroke(s) (if any) are surrounded by L-Bend?
4. Name the strokes without hook?

Write down your own questions.
Feel free to describe and illustrate in your own way.

My Questions:

My Imagination of the Strokes

Use your imagination, what do the **five members in Mr L-Bend's family** remind you of?

Create your own sketchbook! Add clippings. Doodle, Make Notes, Summarise . . .

Meet Mr L7-Bends' Family

(A) L7-Bends

L7-Bends starts with **L-Bend** and ends with **7-Bend or 7-Hook**

1) L7-Bends

L-Bend merges with **7-Bend**. Its two sharp bends are 90º

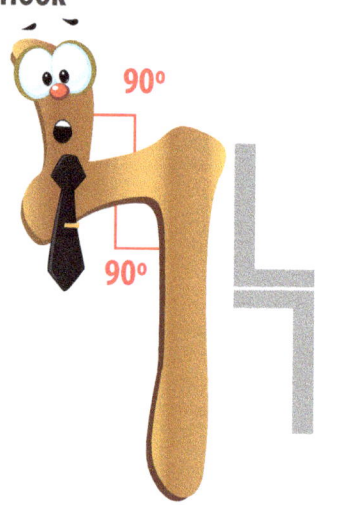

90º

90º

90º

90º

2) L7-Hook

L-Bend merges with **7-Hook.** Its two sharp bends are 90ºand has a left hook

(B) Acute-L7

Acute-L merges with **Acute-7**

< 90º

< 90º

3) Lightning

Its sharp bends are less than 90º (acute angle) and it looks like lightning.

Activity 8
L7-Hook and Acute-L7

Observe how L7-Hook and Acute-L7 vary in width and height in these characters. Identify where the L7-Hook and Acute-L7 comes from. Draw a line to match the character to the stroke.

夷　亏　弓　引　与

与　勹　乛

转　专

勹

厶

L7-Hook and Acute-L7

1. Observe how each stroke appears in different characters? What are the <u>relative lengths</u> of the horizontal and vertical parts?

2. Measure the <u>angles of the two bends</u> in each stroke using a protractor?

My Reflection

Write down your own questions.
Feel free to describe and illustrate in your own

My Questions:

My Imagination of the Strokes

Use your imagination, what do the **three members in Mr L7-Bends' family** remind you of?

Create your own sketchbook! Add clippings. Doodle, Make Notes, Summarise . . .

Meet Mr 7L-Bends' Family

(A) 7L-Bends

7L-Bends starts with **7-Bend** and ends with **L-Bend, Round L or L-Hook**.

1) 7L-Bends

Its two sharp bends are 90º

2) Round-7L

7-Bend merges with **Round-L**. It has one sharp bend and one round bend.

3) 7L-Hook

7-Bend merges with **L-Hook**. It has one sharp bend, one round bend and a hook.

(B) Acute-7L

Acute-7L starts with **Acute-7**

4) Z-Hook

Acute-7 merges with **L-Hook**. Its bends are acute angles and its shape looks like alphabet Z. It has one sharp bend, one round bend and a hook.

Activity 9
7L-Hook and 7-Leanback

This activity is an easy one. 7L-Hook and 7-Leanback look very similar. Identify where the 7L-Hook and 7-Leanback come from. Write the alphabet in the bracket.

L-Hook and 7-Leanback

1. Why do you think 7L-Hook and 7-Leanback are classified in different families even though they look very similar?

2. If you have a compass, draw circles such that their arcs fit into the curve of 7-Leanback (as shown on page 25).
Use something round (e.g. bottle caps of different sizes) if a compass is not available.

3. Which 7-Leanback has the biggest circle?

My Reflection

Write down your own questions.
Feel free to describe and illustrate in your own

My Questions:

My Imagination of the Strokes

Use your imagination, what do the **four members in Mr 7L-Bends' family** remind you of?

Create your own sketchbook! Add clippings.
Doodle, Make Notes, Summarise . . .

Meet Mr Double-7 Bends' Family

(A) Double-7 Bends
7-Bend or Acute-7 merges with 7-Bend, 7-Hook or 7-Slash

1) Double-7 Bends
Two 7-Bends merged together

2) Double-7 Hook
Acute-7 merges with 7-Hook

3) Double-7 Slash
Acute 7 merges with 7-Slash

(B) Acute-7 Hunchback
Acute-7 merges with Hunchback

4) Acute-7 Hunchback

Activity 10
7-Slash and Double-7 Bends

Like RL-Slash, 7-Slash slants at different angles to the horizontal. Identify where the 7-Slash and Double-7 Bends come from.

Draw a line to match the character to the stroke.

多 冬 又 多

乃 队 及 凸 廷

7-Slash and Double-7 Bends

1. Measure the <u>angle of bend</u> of all the strokes.

2. Measure the <u>angle to horizontal</u> of 7-Slash and Double-7 Slash.

3. For 7-Slash and Double-7 Slash, measure where it intersects or touches another stroke. How far is it from its tail or head?

Write down your own questions.
Feel free to describe and illustrate in your own

My Questions:

My Imagination of the Strokes

Use your imagination, what do the **four members in Mr Double-7-Bends' family** remind you of?

Create your own sketchbook! Add clippings.
Doodle, Make Notes, Summarise . . .

Activity 11

a) Highlight *7-Bend* in these characters:

枣 互 丑 唐 兼 典 舆

b) Highlight *L7-Hook*

骂

Highlight *7-Hook* :

Example: 司

咢 写 弟 号 弯 考

c) Highlight *7 Hook* in these characters:

却 那 厉 丽 局 册

Learn Chinese Without Writing © 2015 by W.Q. BLOSH

d) Highlight *Double-7 Hook* :

奶 汤 隽 秀

These tasks are easy. The purpose is to observe how these strokes appear in characters. Compare how differently they look in different characters.

Activity 12

a) Highlight *Acute 7* in these characters:

了 乏 今 甬 角 予 学

b) Highlight *L-Bend* :

收 击 匹 出

c) Highlight *Acute-L* :

台 允 玄

框 每 发

流 亥 参

d) Highlight *7-Slash* in these characters:

友 受 最 麦 处 复 夜

Learn Chinese Without Writing © 2015 by W.Q. BLOSH

Learn Chinese *without* WRITING　**55**

a) Highlight *7-Leanback* :

b) Highlight
L-Hook:

c) Highlight
7L-Hook :

d) Highlight
Z-Hook:

e) Highlight
7-Back kick:

飞 虱 汽 凤 氖 迅
犯 记 旨 见 先 光 兔
冗 亮 凡 秃 瓷 究 赢
艺 疗
话

Learn Chinese Without Writing © 2015 by W.Q. BLOSH

Activity 14

Have you been paying attention to their names? Test your memory. Do not turn back to earlier pages. Match the highlighted stroke to its name. See example. Each name can be linked more than once.

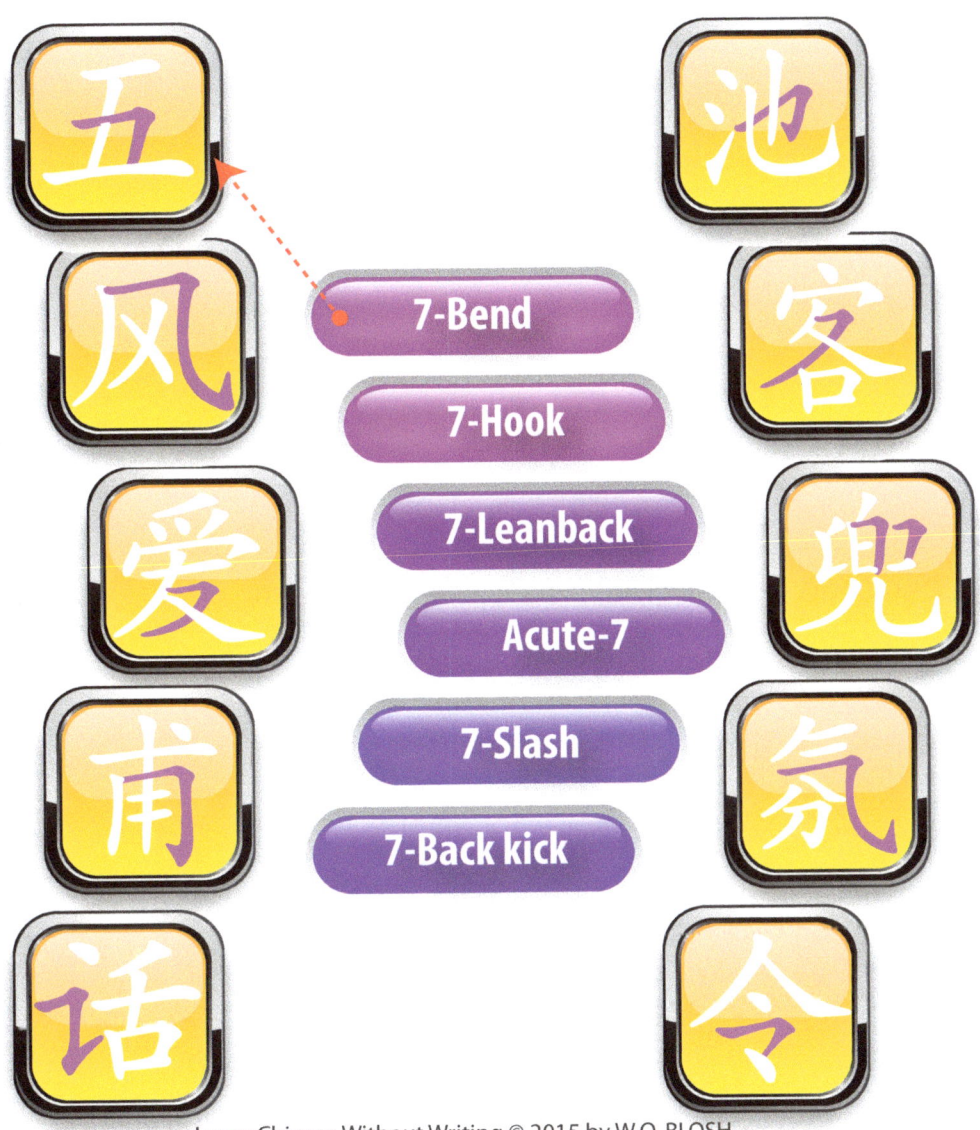

7-Bend

7-Hook

7-Leanback

Acute-7

7-Slash

7-Back kick

Learn Chinese Without Writing © 2015 by W.Q. BLOSH

Activity 15

Test your memory. Do not turn back to earlier pages. Match the highlighted stroke to its name. Each name can be linked more than once.

Round-7L

7L-Bends

7L-Hook

Z-Hook

Double-7 Bends

Double-7 Hook

Double-7 Slash

Acute-7 Hunchback

Learn Chinese Without Writing © 2015 by W.Q. BLOSH

Activity 16

Test your memory. Do not turn back to earlier pages. Match the highlighted stroke to its name. Each name can be linked more than once.

L-Hook

L-Bend

Round-L

Boomerang

Acute-L

L7-Bends

L7-Hook

Acute-L7

Learn Chinese Without Writing © 2015 by W.Q. BLOSH

Common Features of Strokes

	STROKE FAMILIES			
	STRAIGHT	CURVE	DOT	BEND
1. Hook	✓	✓		✓
2. Angle to Horizontal	✓	✓	✓	
3. Angle of Bend				✓
4. Arc of Circle		✓		

FEATURES

Fonts

In this book, most of the characters use the font 'Kaiti' which is more like calligraphic writing and closer to handwriting. Characters in this font have 'shapely figures' and provide more details than stick-like characters. Observe the different parts of each stroke ... see how it becomes fatter or thinner, or tapers off ...

tapers off

Kaiti   **Songti**   **Heiti**

3

Adapt
Balance
Centre

2

Apart
Bonding
Crossing

1

Angles
Bends
Curves

Triple
ABCs
Concept

Apart

Performers not touching one another

Section 2

Apart

Bonding

Crossing

Bonding

At least one part of a performer touches another performer

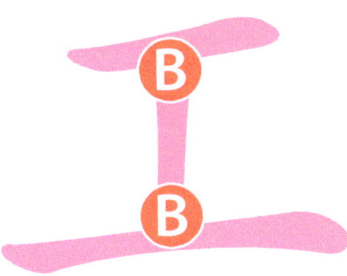

Crossing

At least two performers intersecting each other

Formations

The second set of ABC (Apart, Bonding, Crossing) explains how characters (formations) are created and explains the relationships between the strokes (performers).

1.
Apart

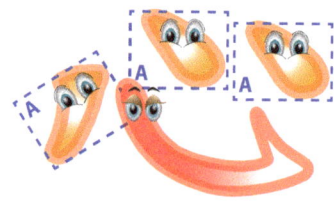

2.
Bonding

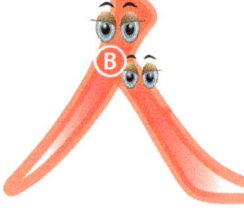

3.
Crossing

Apart

Strokes not touching one another

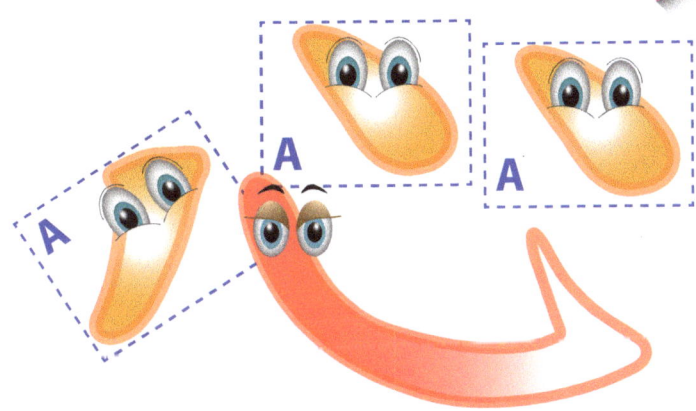

Apart

Some characters are made up of strokes not touching one another but are positioned relative to one another. Take note of how the strokes are spaced apart to ensure that the characters look balanced and centred.

1. Equal Space Between Parallel Strokes

2. Dots Spaced Evenly

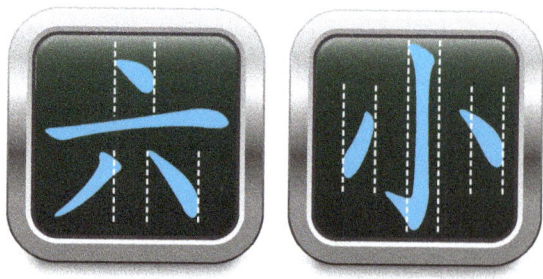

3. Placed at Mid-point

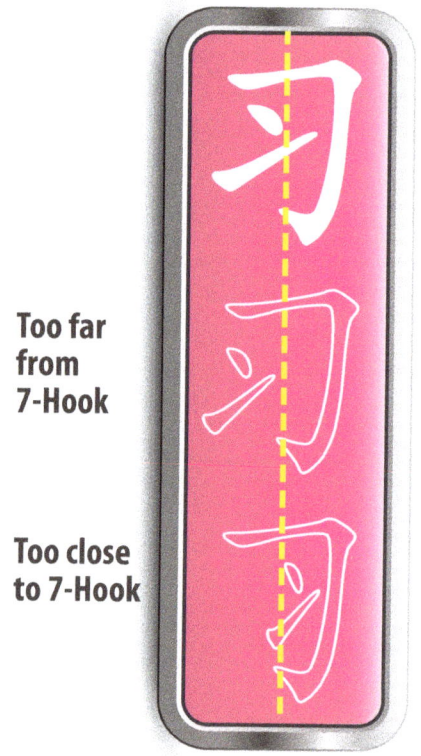

Too far from 7-Hook

Too close to 7-Hook

Dot and Tick should not be too far or too close to 7-Hook

4. Positioning of Multiple Dots

As dots are often apart from other strokes, it is important to observe how they are positioned relative to other strokes. Here is an example on how to analyse dots.

a) Curl-up Positioned with Respect to the Left Dot
The starting point of Curl-up is slightly below the starting point of the left dot.

b) Artistic Positioning
The three dots are positioned artistically at different heights with the middle dot at the highest point.

Highest

Middle

Lowest

c) Spacing Evenly
The three dots are spaced evenly horizontally.

d) Dots Positioned Relative to Curl-up
The dots are not positioned too close or too far from the Curl-up

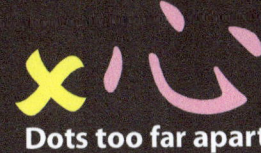

Dots too close

Dots too far apart

Apart Examples

All these characters are made up of strokes not touching one another. Observe carefully how the strokes are spaced apart from one another. Draw lines to dissect the characters to analyse the spaces between the strokes. See examples on previous pages.

Bonding

At least one part of a stroke touches another stroke.

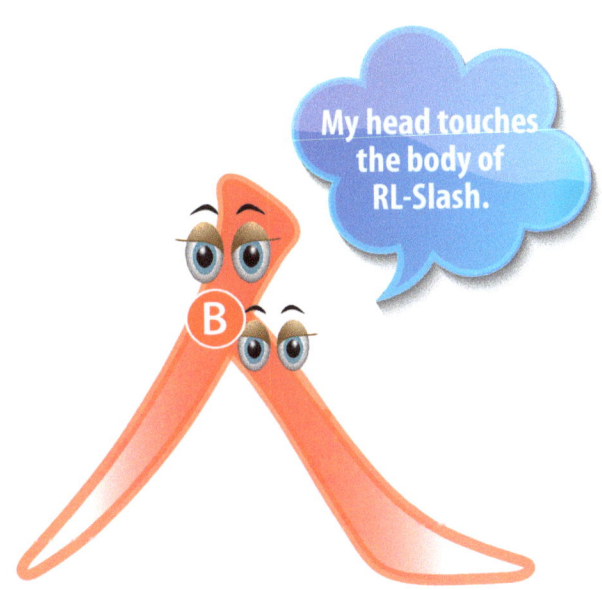

Bonding

The second way how strokes are combined is through 'Bonding', that is a stroke touches another stroke at one point. There should not be any gap between the strokes and neither should they be overlapping each other. See pictures.

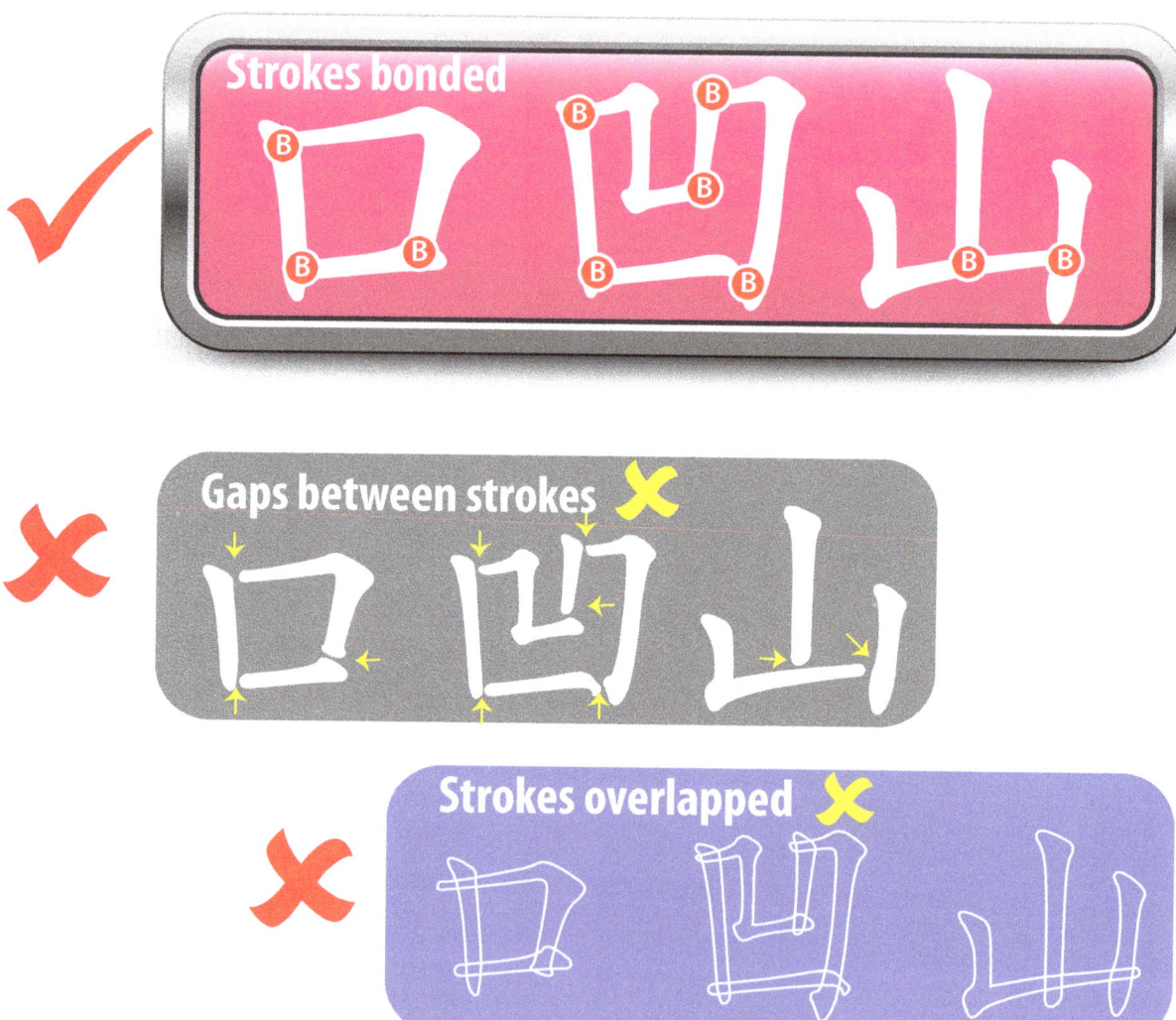

Types of Bonding

A 'Head-Head (HH)' bonding occurs when the **start** of an earlier stroke touches the **start** of a latter stroke.
A 'Head-Tail (TT)' bonding occurs when the **start** of an earlier stroke touches the **end** of a latter stroke.

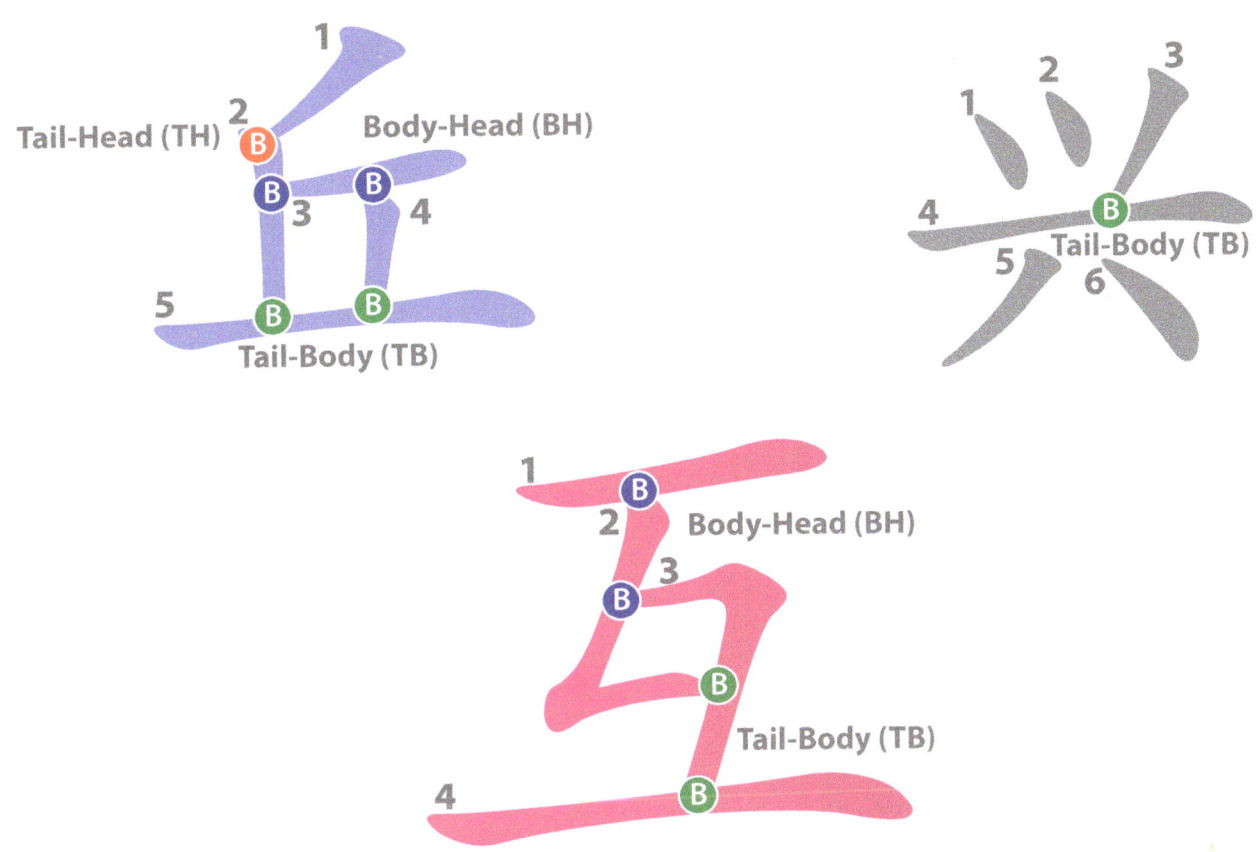

Bonding occurs when any of its parts—the head (H), body (B) and tail (T) of a stroke touches one of these parts of another stroke. The only exception is 'Body-Body' interaction, which is a crossing not bonding.

Activity 17 Bond Points

In the shaded characters, indicate the **Bond Points** using the 'B' symbol.
Even though you have not learnt these characters, you will be able to identify the bond points easily. Some clues are given in the outlined characters.

Crossing

At least two strokes intersecting each other.

Crossing: Different Meanings

English
In English, it is not wrong to mix up bonding and crossing. You can write the strokes as just touching or overlapping slightly.

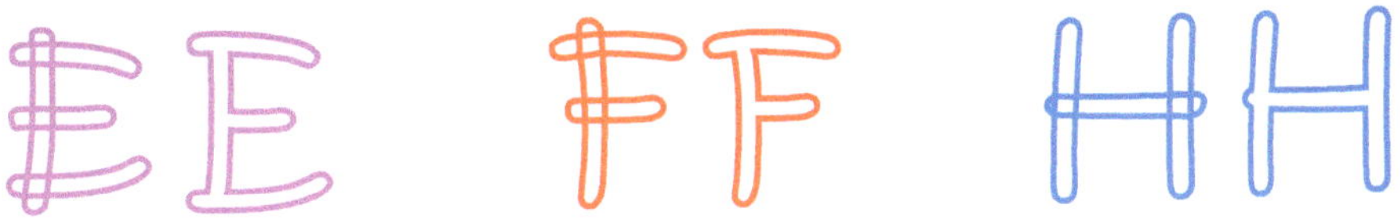

EE FF HH

Chinese
However, in Chinese even a slight overlap matters. Observe the difference between each pair of characters. The characters may look identical to you, but they are very different and have totally different meanings.

刀 力
Knife **Strength**

午 牛
Noon **Cow**

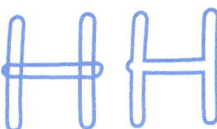
田 由
Field **Caused by**

天 夫
Sky **Man; Husband**

矢 失
Arrow **Lose**

开 井
Open **(Water) Well**

Activity 18
Cross Points

Indicate the **Cross Points** in the shaded characters using the 'C' symbol. See examples.

Combinations of ABC (Apart, Bonding, Crossing)

Observe these characters with different types of ABC combinations. Identifying the **Bond Points (BP)** and **Cross Points (CP)** of a character helps us to notice

* where a stroke starts and ends,
* what is its relationship with other strokes and
* where does the BP or CP occur (e.g. 1/4 length from the head).

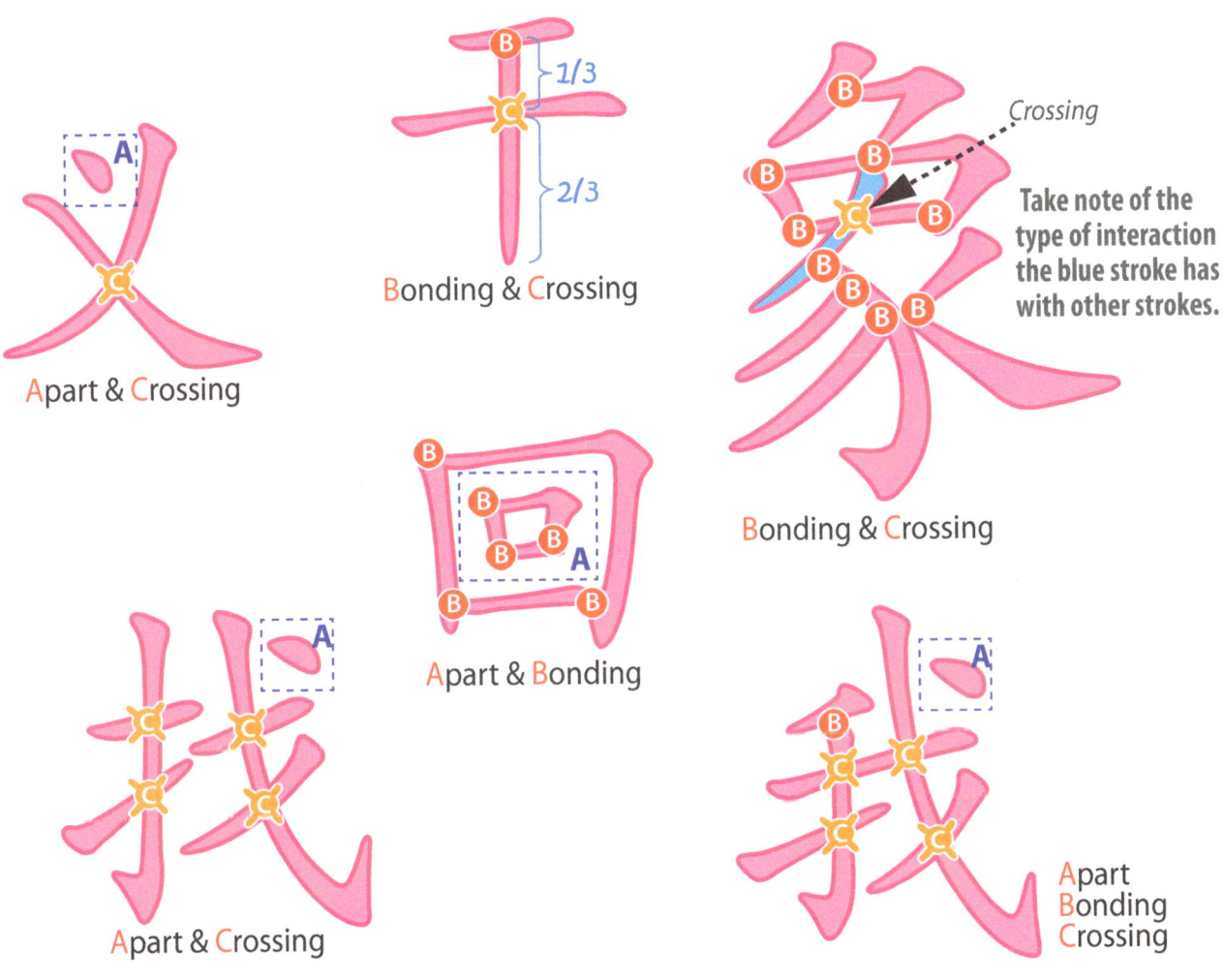

Apart & Crossing

Bonding & Crossing

Apart & Bonding

Bonding & Crossing

Crossing

Take note of the type of interaction the blue stroke has with other strokes.

Apart & Crossing

Apart Bonding Crossing

Activity 19

Combinations of ABC 1

Compare each pair of characters. Indicate the **Bond Points** and **Cross Points** using the given symbols. If the stroke does not touch another stroke, use the **Apart** symbol. See examples.

Apart

A

Bond

B

Cross

C

78 APART, BONDING & CROSSING

Activity 20
Combinations of ABC 2

Indicate the **Bond points** and **Cross points** using the given symbols. If the stroke does not touch another stroke, use the **Apart** symbol.

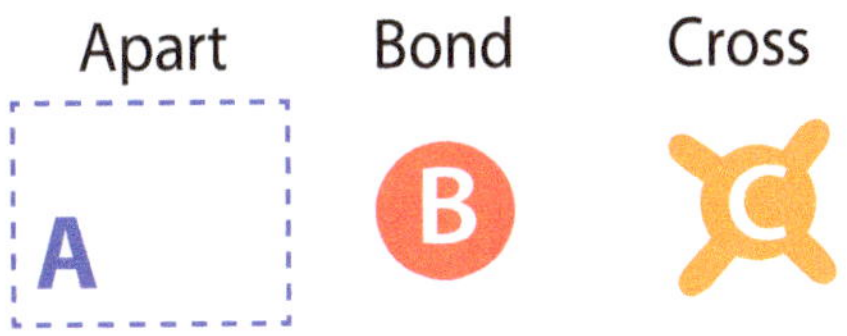

Apart   Bond   Cross

A   B

才　千　斤　发

区　表　丐

狗　鸟　戋

Level of Interactivity

The Level of Interactivity measures how 'friendly' a stroke is.

If more parts of a stroke are possible Bond Points and Cross Points, the easier it is to interact with it.

Bond Anywhere (Vertical)

Discover the level of interactivity of strokes.
- Which parts of a stroke bond/cross most frequently with other strokes
- Which parts of a stroke never bond/cross with other strokes

B Bond point

C Cross point

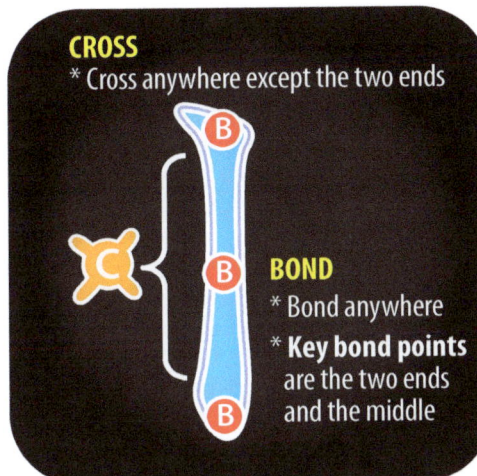

CROSS
* Cross anywhere except the two ends

BOND
* Bond anywhere
* **Key bond points** are the two ends and the middle

For vertical strokes, any part of the stroke can be **Bond Points**, and any part of the stroke except the two ends, can be **Cross Points**.

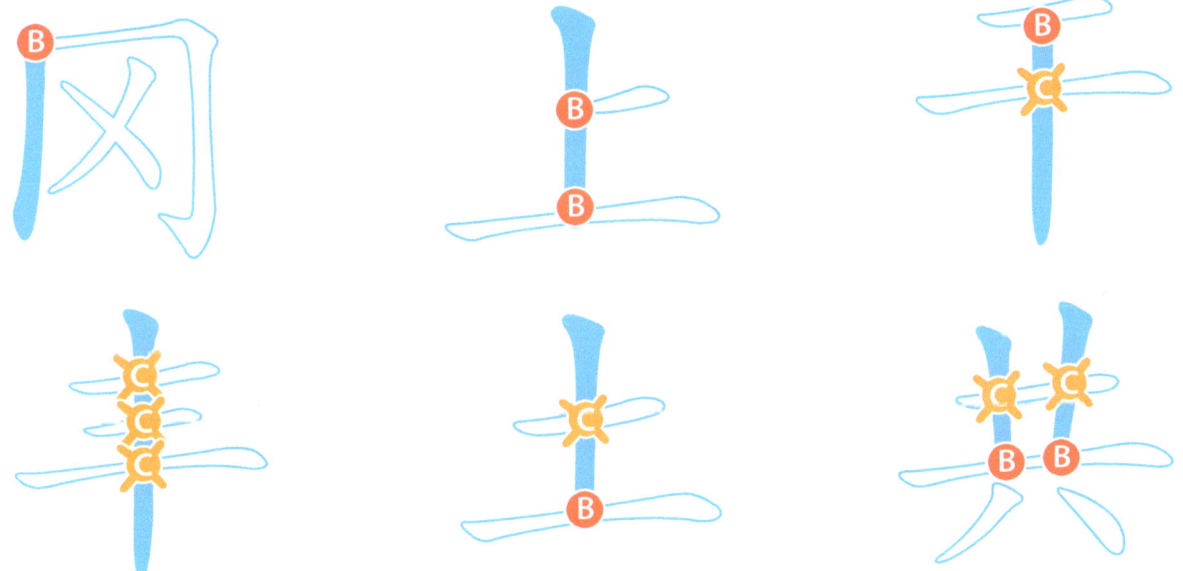

Bond Anywhere (Horizontal)

For horizontal strokes, any part of the stroke can be **Bond Points**, and any part of the stroke except the two ends, can be **Cross Points**.

(B) Bond point

(C) Cross point

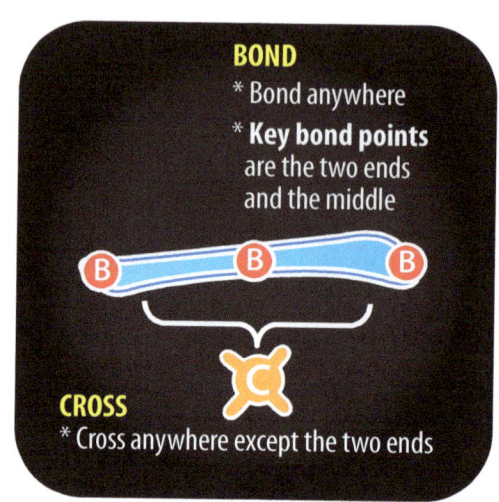

BOND
* Bond anywhere
* **Key bond points** are the two ends and the middle

CROSS
* Cross anywhere except the two ends

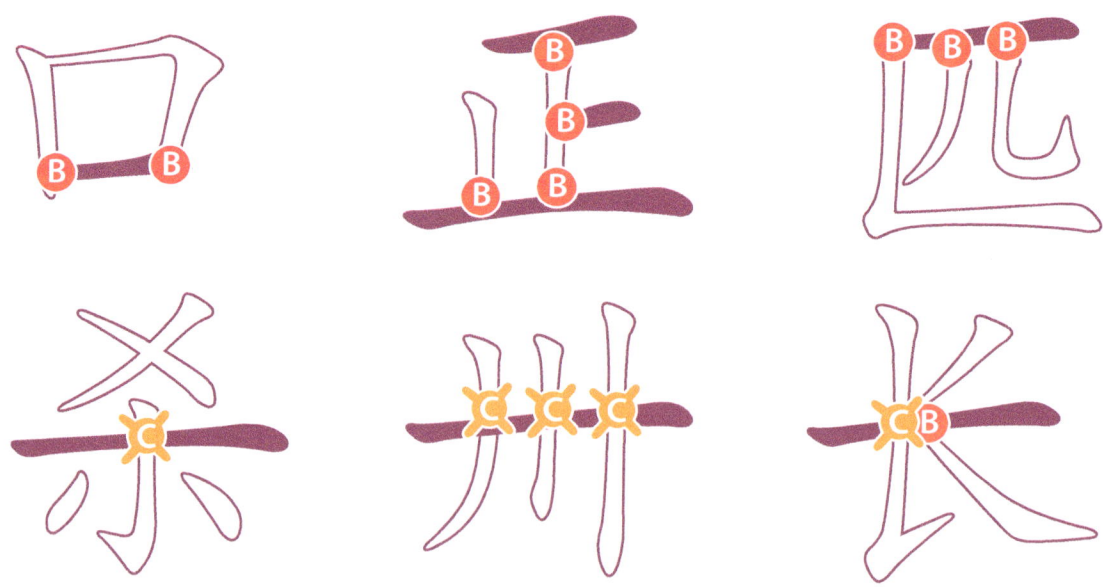

No **B**onding or **C**rossing at Tail (RL-Slash)

For RL-Slashes, **Bond Points** are usually along the upper part of the body. **Cross Points** are also along the upper part of the body except the starting point (head). The tails of slashes are never the bond point or cross point.

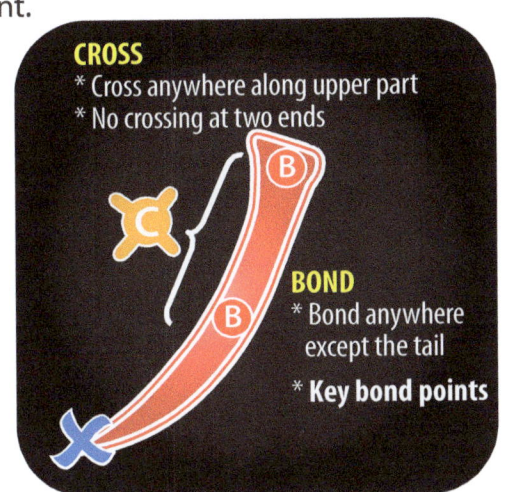

CROSS
* Cross anywhere along upper part
* No crossing at two ends

BOND
* Bond anywhere except the tail

* **Key bond points**

B Bond point

C Cross point

X Point on stroke that does not bond with or cross another stroke.

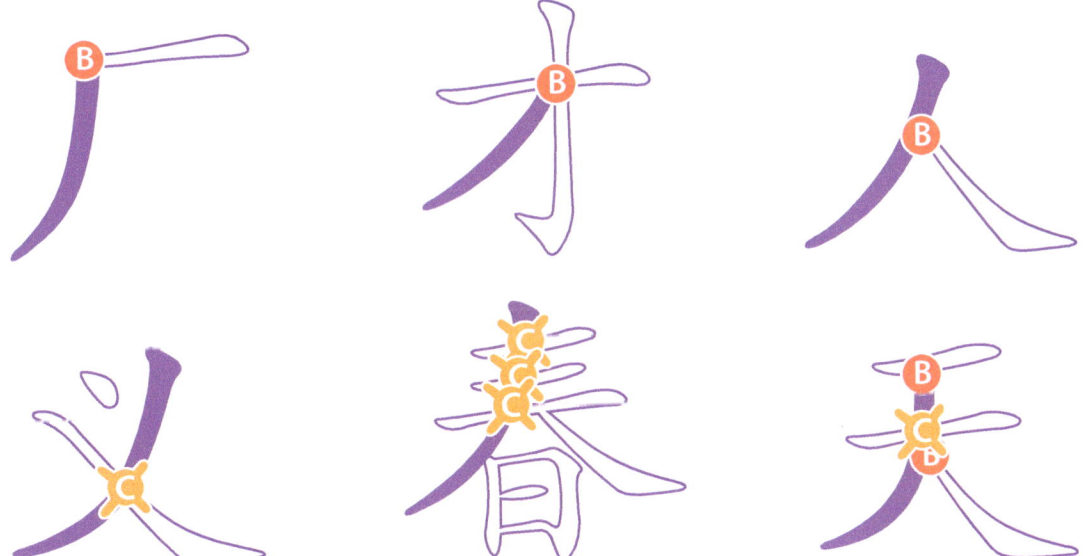

No Bonding or Crossing at Tail (LR-Slash)

For LR-Slashes, **Bond Points** are usually along the upper part of the body. **Cross Points** are also along the upper part of the body except the starting point (head). The tails of slashes are never the bond point or cross point.

B Bond point

C Cross point

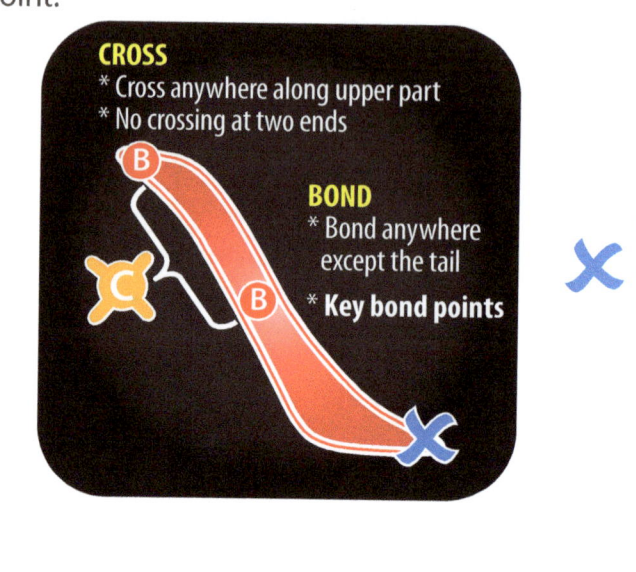

CROSS
* Cross anywhere along upper part
* No crossing at two ends

BOND
* Bond anywhere except the tail

* **Key bond points**

X Point on stroke that does not bond with or cross another stroke.

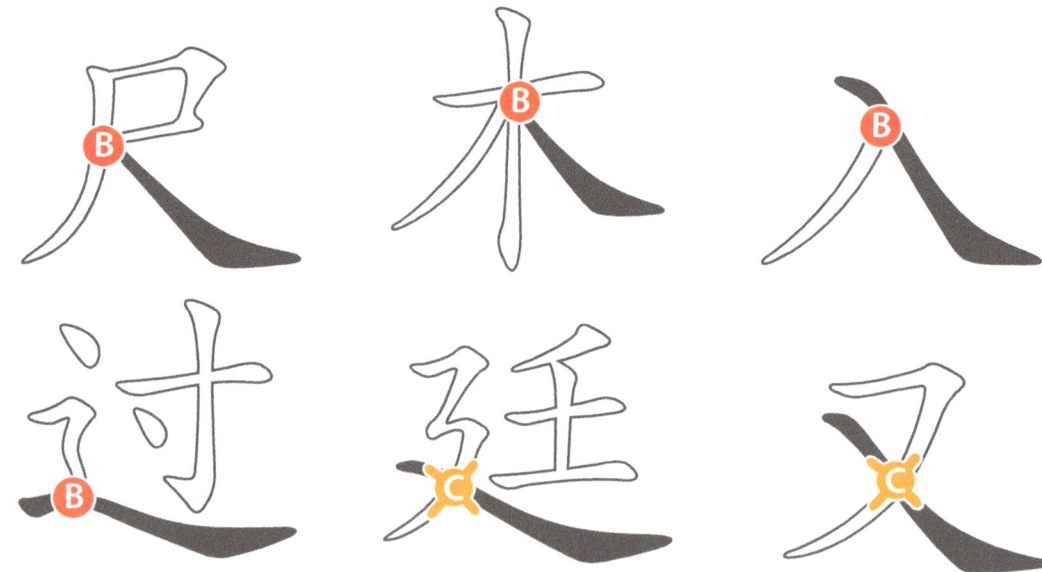

No Bonding or Crossing at Hook
(Hunchback, Leanback, Curl-up)
Bond point and cross point **do not** occur at the hook part of a stroke.

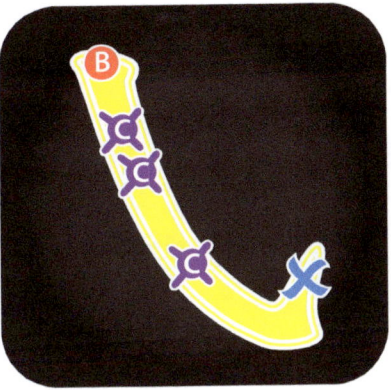

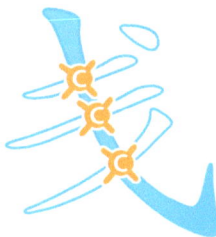

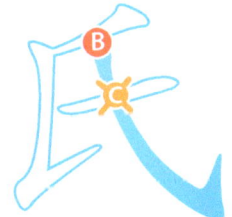

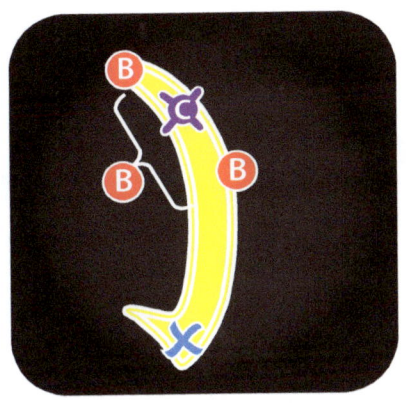 C Key Cross Points	B Key Bond Points	X Point that does not bond or cross with another stroke

 C Key Cross Points   B Key Bond Points   X Point that does not bond or cross with another stroke

No Bonding or Crossing at Bend
(7-Bend, Acute-7, L-Bend and Acute-L)

Bond point and cross point **do not** occur at the bent part of a stroke.

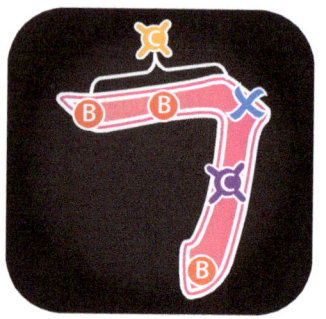 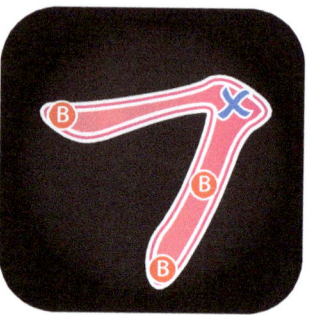 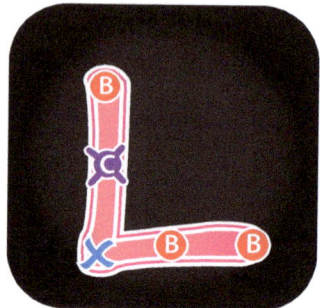 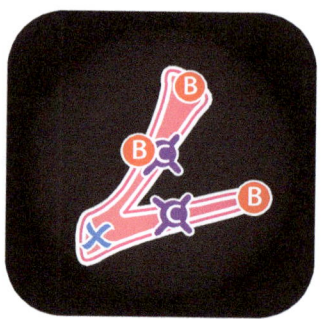

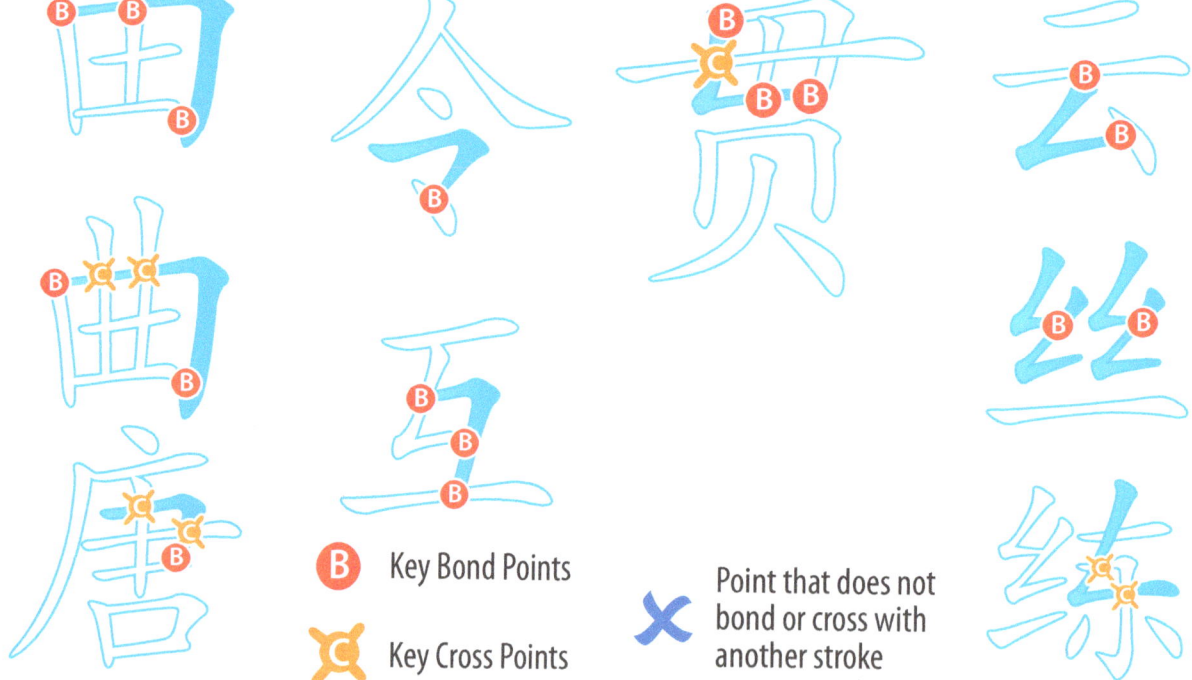

B Key Bond Points

C Key Cross Points

✗ Point that does not bond or cross with another stroke

No Bonding or Crossing at Hook and Bends
(7 Hook, 7-Leanback, 7L-Hook and Double-7 Hook)

Bond point and cross point **do not** occur at the hook or bent parts of a stroke.

 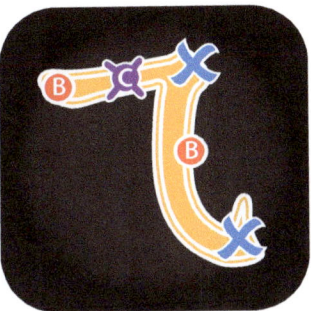 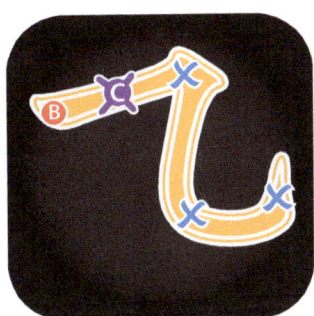 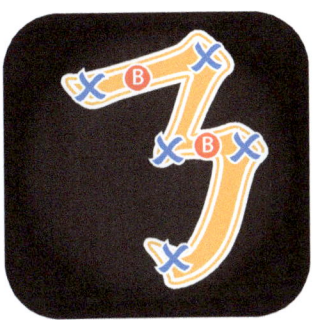

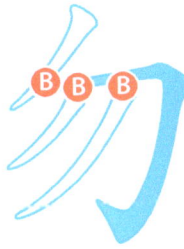 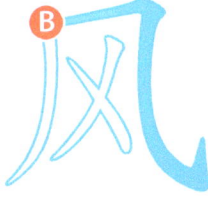  

 Key Cross Points

 Key Bond Points

✕ Point that does not bond or cross with another stroke

Apart, Bonding and Crossing

1. When a stroke crosses another stroke where do they intersect exactly?
   E.g. The CP is 1/4 of its length from the head.

2. Use any characters from Activities 33 to 35, apply what you have learnt
   on Apart, Bonding and Crossing to analyse them.

My Reflection

My Questions:

Do You Recognise Them? ...

Look at their features carefully.

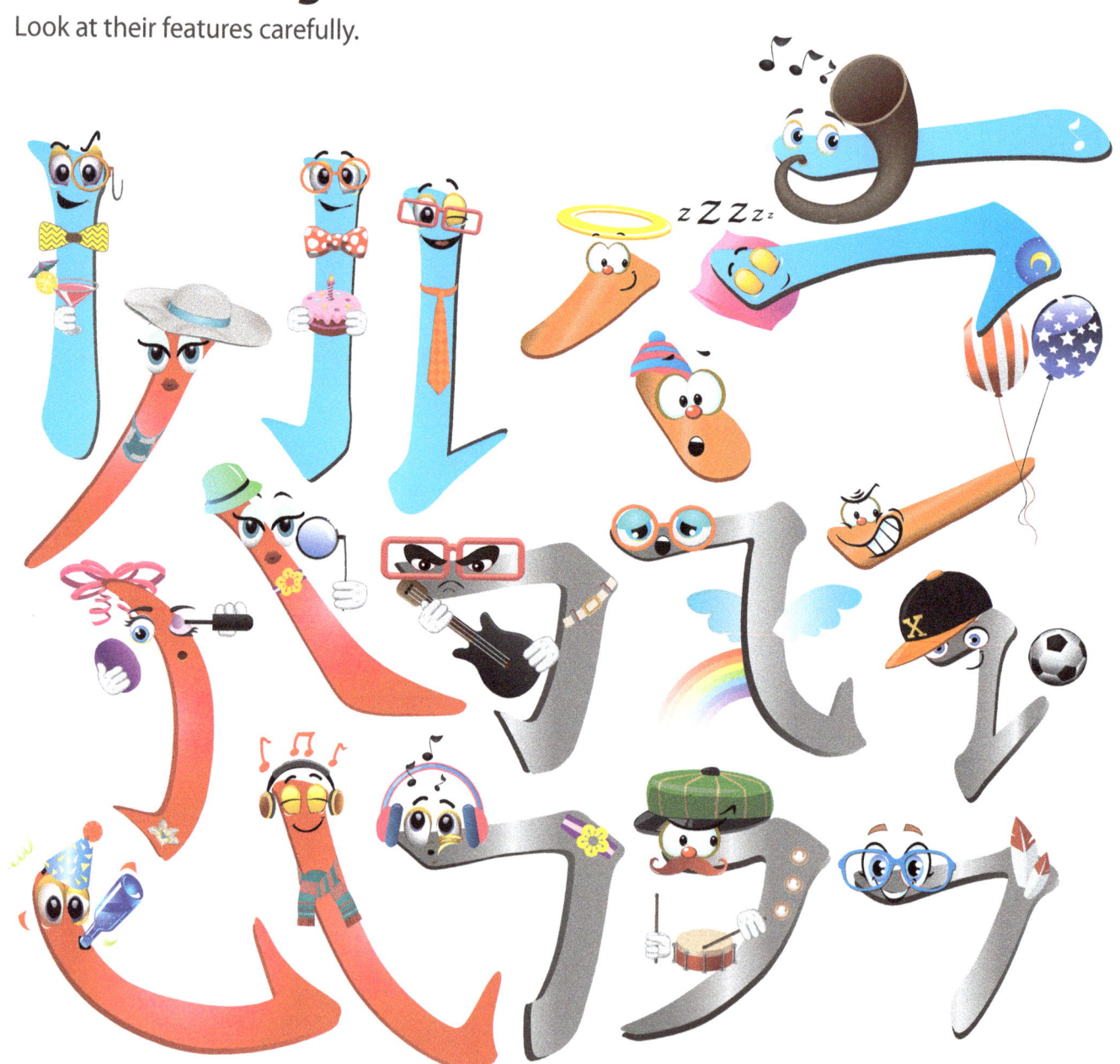

35 Performers

Answer the questions on the next page.

Without turning back to earlier pages, write the name of the stroke. Note that there could be more than one answer.

1. Who has an umbrella? _____

2. Who blows a horn? _____

3. Who has a boomerang? _____

4. Who is putting on eye shadow? _____

5. Who has balloons? _____

6. Who won the first prize? _____

7. Who likes snorkelling? _____

8. Who is struck by lightning? _____

9. Who wears a necklace? _____

10 Who listens to music? _____

11. Who has a magnifying glass? _____

12. Who wears an eye patch? _____

13. Who is drinking from a bottle? _____

14. Who flies with his cap? _____

15. Who flies with wings? _____

After you have checked the answers, revise those names you have made mistakes or forgotten.

3

Adapt
Balance
Centre

2

Apart
Bonding
Crossing

1

Angles
Bends
Curves

Triple
ABCs
Concept

Adapt

a) Size Adaptation

b) Stroke Adaptation

Balance

a) Symmetry

Centre

a) Circle
b) Shape

Write/Draw this character in the box.

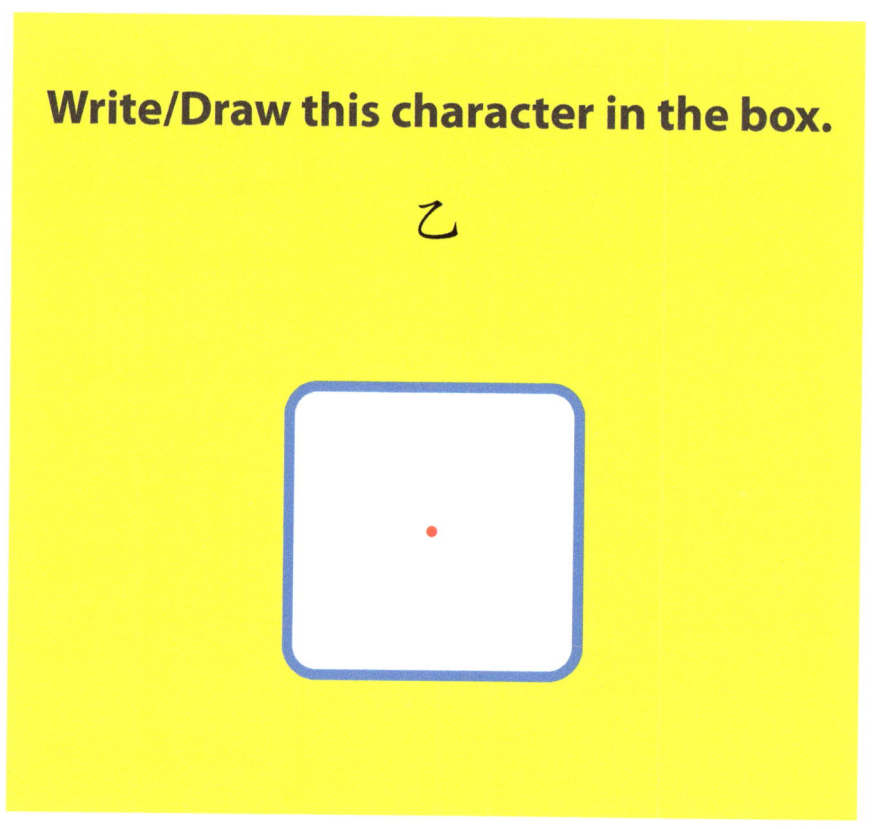

Performance Techniques

The third set of ABC (Adapt, Balance and Centre) explains how the strokes (performers) should perform so that aesthetic requirements of Chinese characters (formations) could be met.

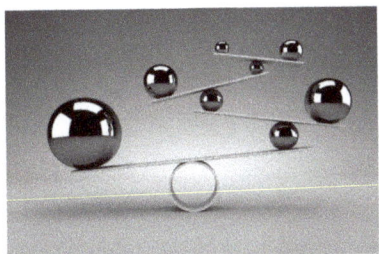

The Box Stage

Box Stage

The performers perform on a square stage. They have to cooperate with other performers to create a beautiful formation within this limited space. They have to learn to **a**dapt, **b**alance and **c**entre themselves so that the formation will look good.

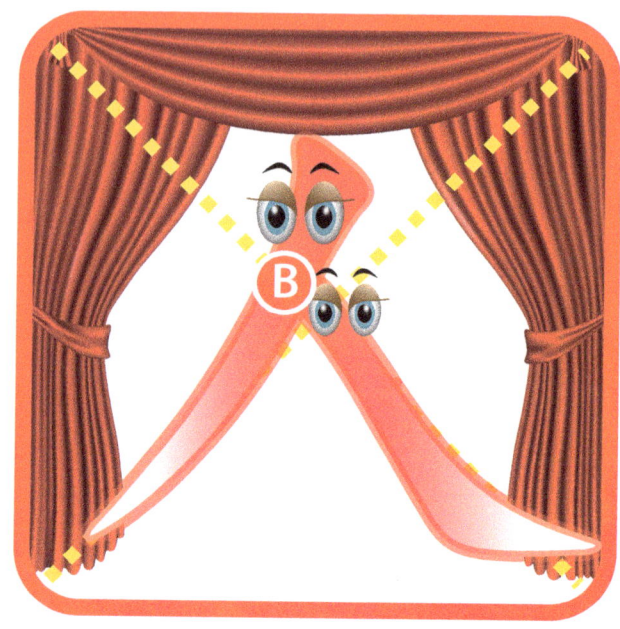

Imaginery Lines

The job is not easy so the performers have to find some ways to help themselves. During rehearsals, the performers will train with lines strung across the stage so they know the exact positions they have to be.

In actual performance, these lines have to be removed so performers have to imagine these lines in their mind. These are called the Imaginery Lines.

Basic Structures

Similar to creating formations on a box stage, Chinese characters are created within a square box. The dotted lines (imaginery lines) in the box divide the square box into different spaces. Here are the basic structures of characters.

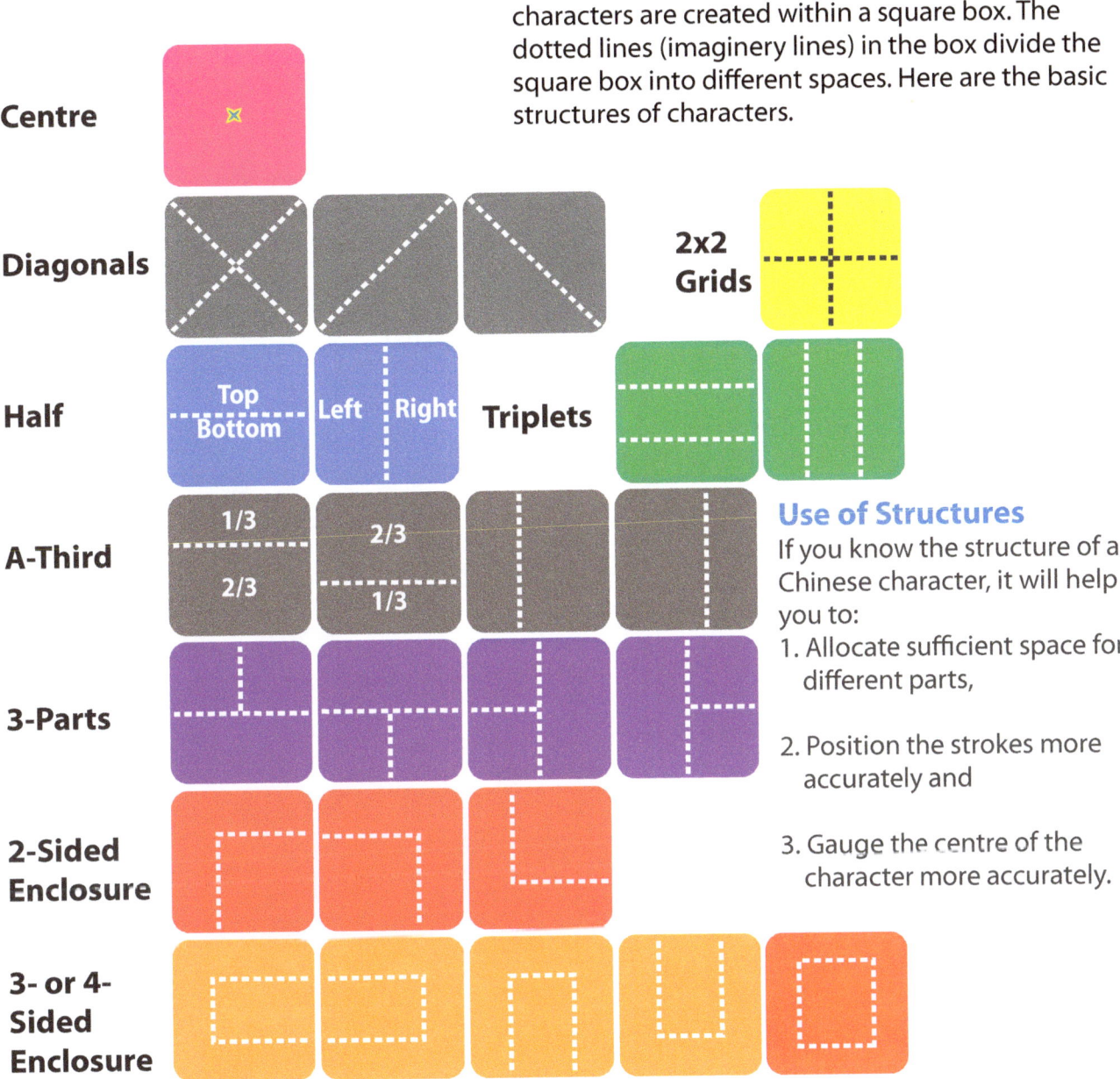

Centre

Diagonals

2x2 Grids

Half — Top / Bottom, Left | Right — **Triplets**

A-Third — 1/3, 2/3, 2/3, 1/3

3-Parts

2-Sided Enclosure

3- or 4-Sided Enclosure

Use of Structures

If you know the structure of a Chinese character, it will help you to:

1. Allocate sufficient space for different parts,

2. Position the strokes more accurately and

3. Gauge the centre of the character more accurately.

Fitting into Structures

Centre

Centre and 4-sided Enclosure

Observe how the characters fit into these structures so that they look balanced and centred.

Notice how the strokes align to the 'imaginery lines'.

Diagonals

45° 45°

义

尺

戈

夕

2x2 Grids

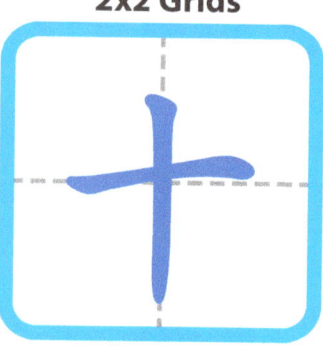

王

垂

大

米

Diagonals and 2x2 Grids combined

Same Structure Different Characters

Observe how characters of different levels of complexity fit into the two types of 'Half' structures.

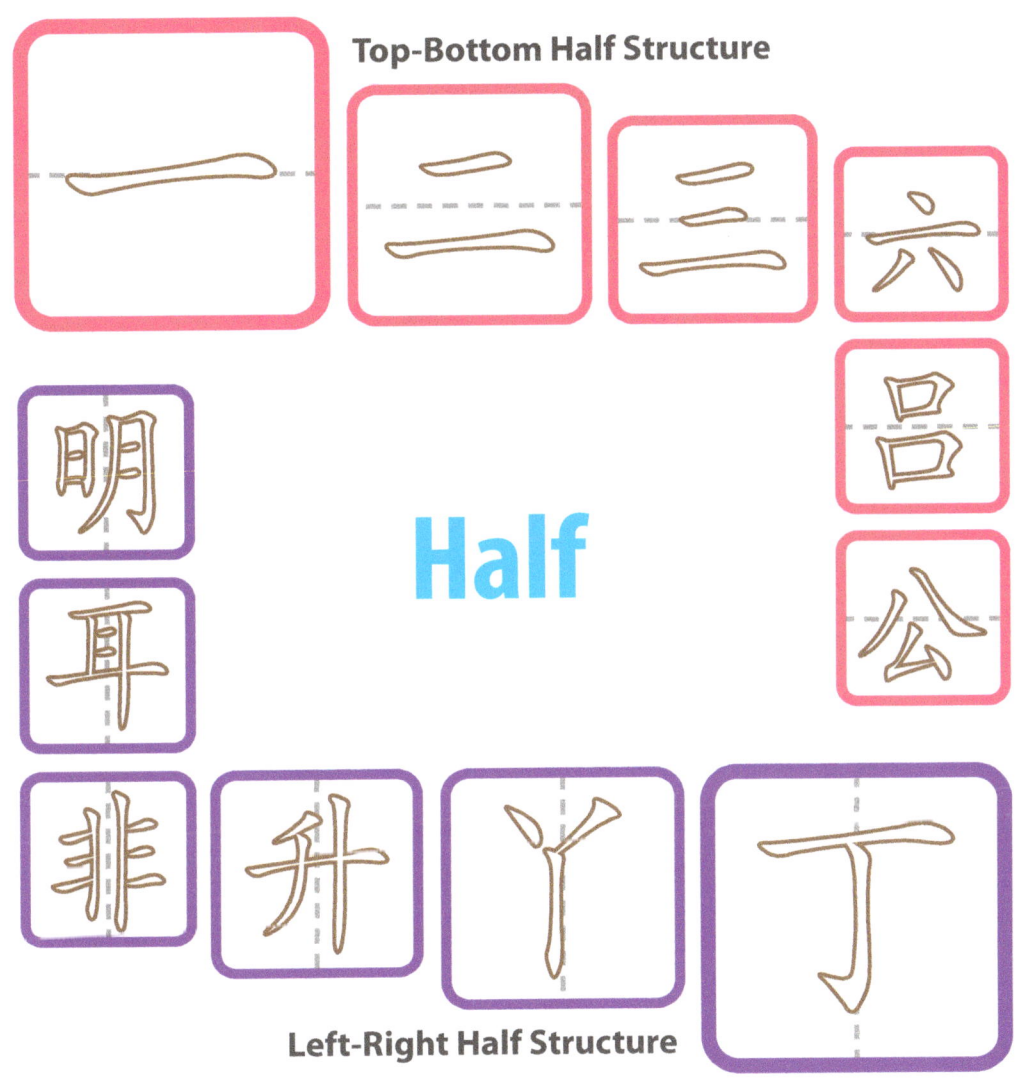

Top-Bottom Half Structure

Half

Left-Right Half Structure

n-Sided Structures

It is easy to recognise characters that have 2, 3 or 4-sided structures. The frame (outer layer) encloses the inner part on 2, 3 or 4 sides respectively.

(A) 2-Sided

L-Frame

7-Frame

Inverse-7-Frame

(B) 3-Sided

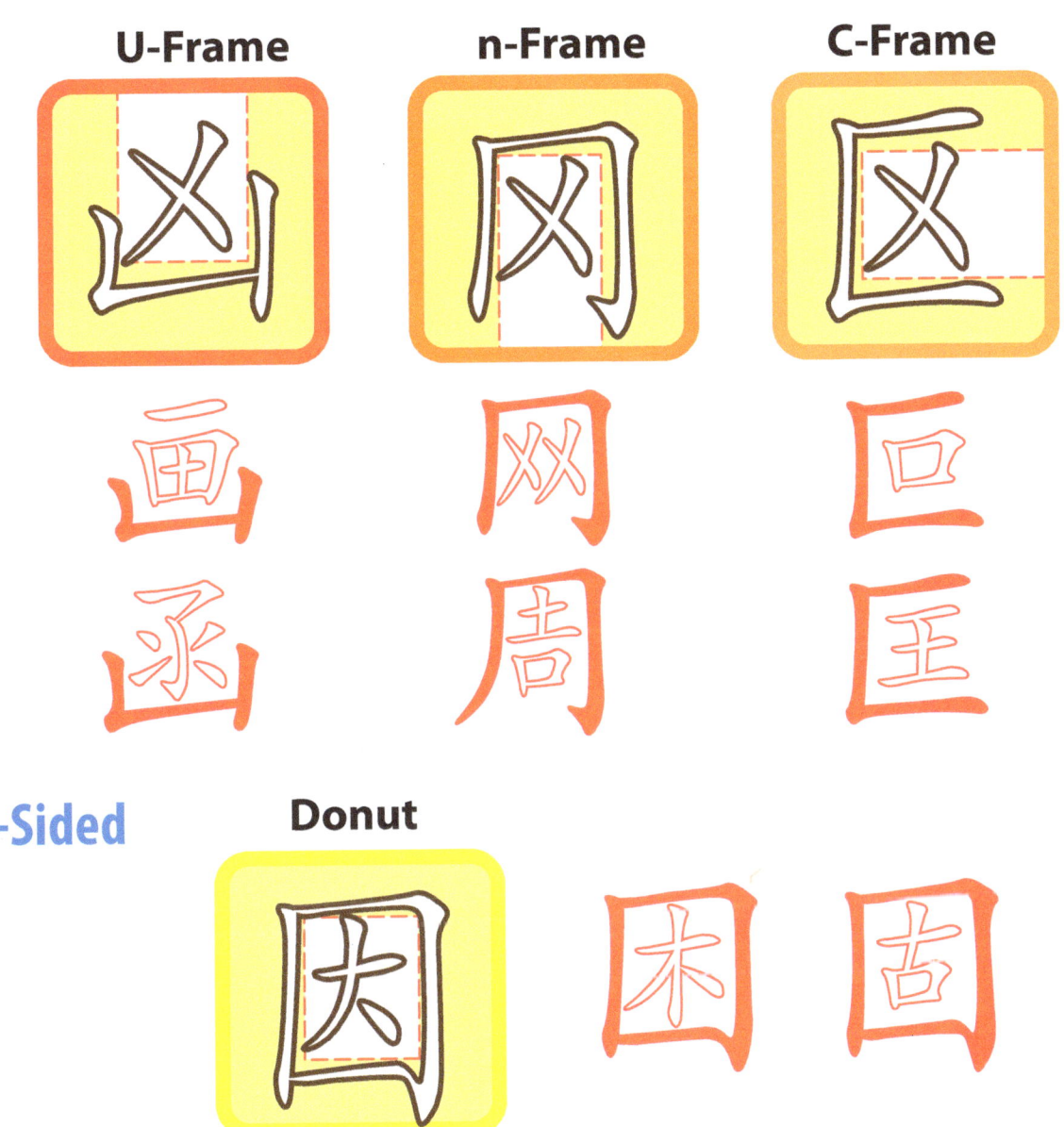

U-Frame **n-Frame** **C-Frame**

(C) 4-Sided

Donut

Activity 22 Basic Structures

Look at the characters carefully and see which structures they fit in. Write the alphabet (a) to (p) in the given brackets.

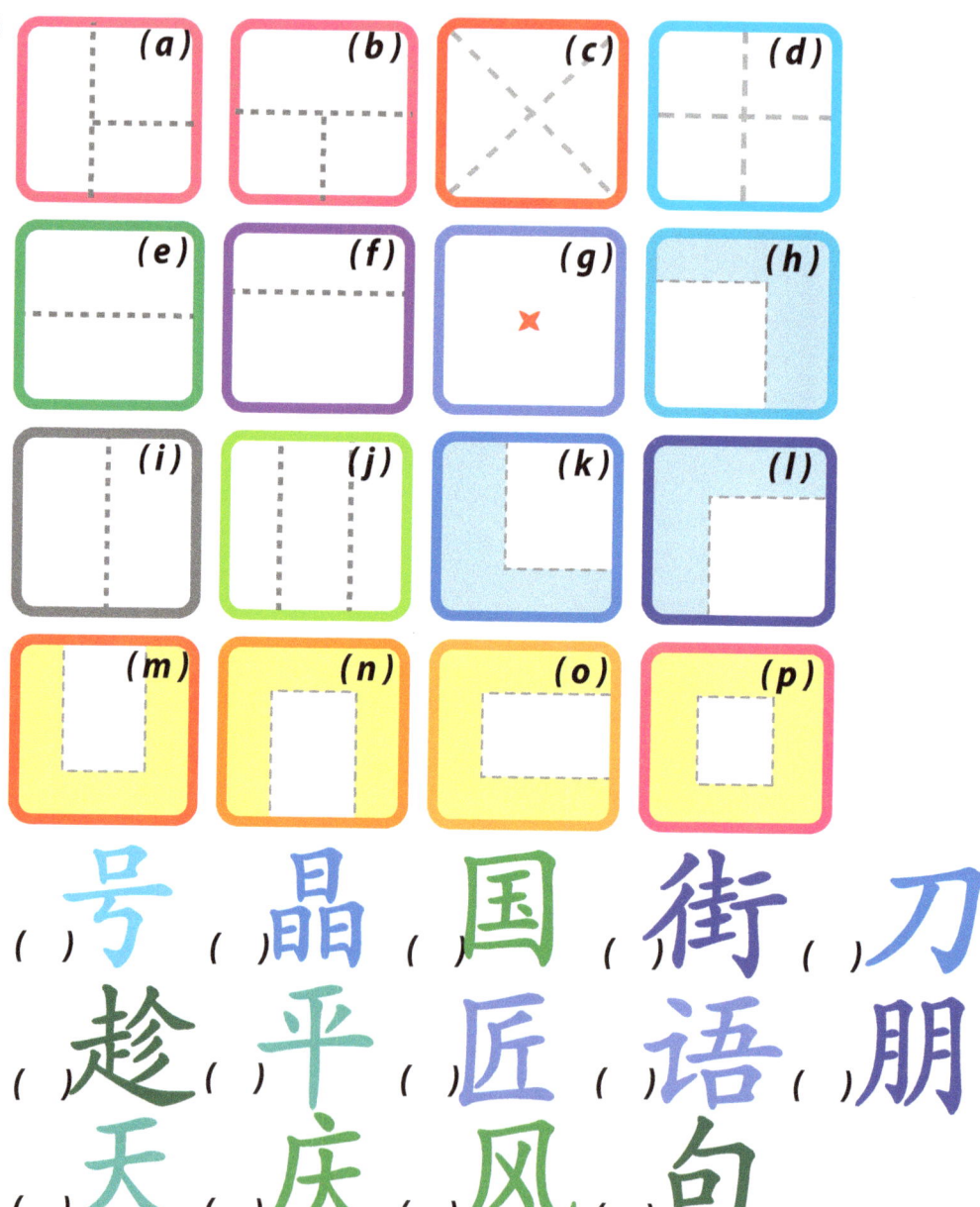

( ) 函 ( ) 号 ( ) 晶 ( ) 国 ( ) 街 ( ) 刀

( ) 吉 ( ) 趁 ( ) 平 ( ) 匠 ( ) 语 ( ) 朋

( ) 天 ( ) 庆 ( ) 风 ( ) 句

Adapt

Water is highly adaptable. It takes on the shape of its container.

Adapt

The performers (strokes) are also very versatile. They can transform themselves by changing the size of their formation (character) or by changing the length of performer (stroke).

Size Adaptation

1. Flatten
2. Slim down
3. Shrink

Stroke Adaptation

1. Stretch
2. Shorten
3. Change Angle
4. Transform

Types of Size Adaptation

See how each character can change its size by slimming down, flattening or shrinking itself.

1. Flatten

Change in height

3. Shrink

Change in width and height

2. Slim Down

Change in width

When a character **flattens**, there is a big change in **height** but little or no change in width.

When a character **slims down**, there is a big change in **width** but little or no change in height.

When a character **shrinks**, both its **height and width** change.

Size Adaptation Evolution

Flatten   Shrink

Observe how the a character **flattens, slims down** or **shrinks** to fit into characters with different structures.

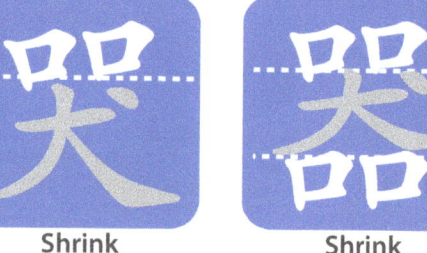 

Shrink   Shrink   Shrink

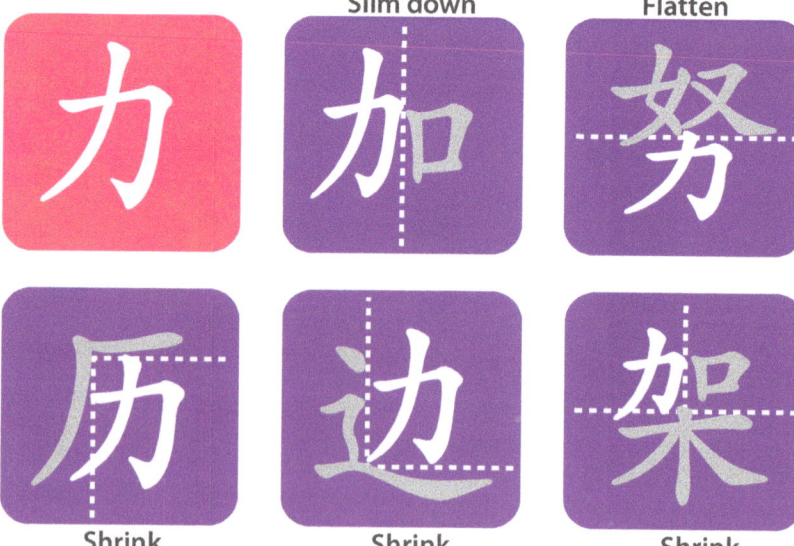

Slim down   Flatten

Shrink   Shrink   Shrink

Simple to Complex

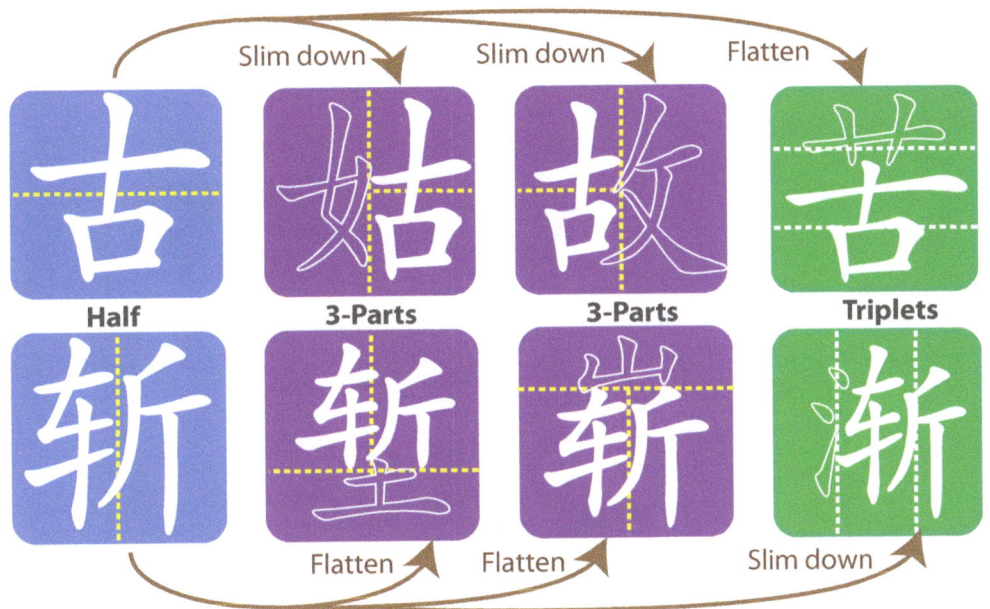

Slim down   Slim down   Flatten

Half   **3-Parts**   **3-Parts**   **Triplets**

Flatten   Flatten   Slim down

The above characters show how a character in a 'Half' structure can fit into a '3-parts' and 'Triplets' structures by slimming down or flattening. As a character incorporates itself into another character, the structure of the latter character becomes more complex.

Below is another example of a character incorporating into other characters. The structures of these characters are shown below them. Draw the imaginery lines on the characters:

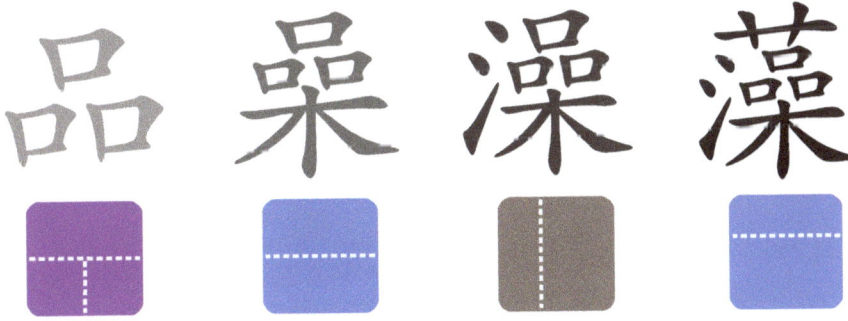

Complex to Simple

Decoding Complex Characters

Some characters do not fit into the basic structures shown. Analyse them by breaking them into two or more basic structures.

This character can be broken down into two 'Triplets' structure (vertical and horizontal).

These characters can be broken down into two basic structures. Draw the imaginery lines on the characters:

These characters can be broken down into two basic structures. One structure is incorporated into the other structure. Draw the imaginery lines on the characters:

Adaptation Example 1

See how versatile this character is. Observe how it makes

a) Size Adaptation or

b) Stroke Adaptation or

c) Both

to fit into different characters.

人

LR-Slash stretches horizontally

RL-Slash stretches vertically

Slim down	Shrink	Flatten		
认	坠	盒	赶	爽

Shorten LR-Slash and

Slant

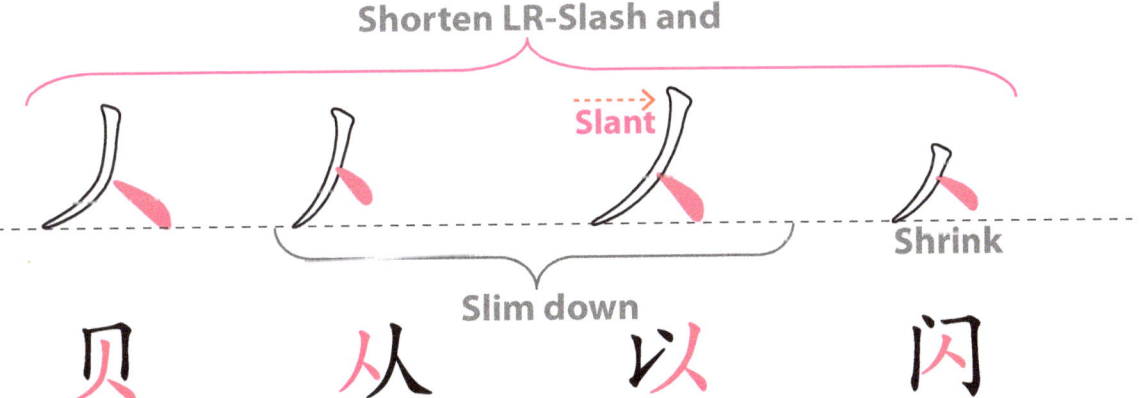

Slim down

Shrink

贝   从   以   闪

Adaptation Example 2

More examples on how versatile these characters are.

Flatten
究

Slim down
轨

7L-Hook stretches horizontally
旭

7L-Hook transforms into
7-Back kick   **7-Leanback**

Shrink
鸠

Slim down
执

L-Hook transforms into
Vertical Right Hook

Slim down
玩

Flatten
完

Shrink
园

Slim down
顽

L-Hook stretches horizontally
冠

Adaptation Example 3

See how versatile these character are.

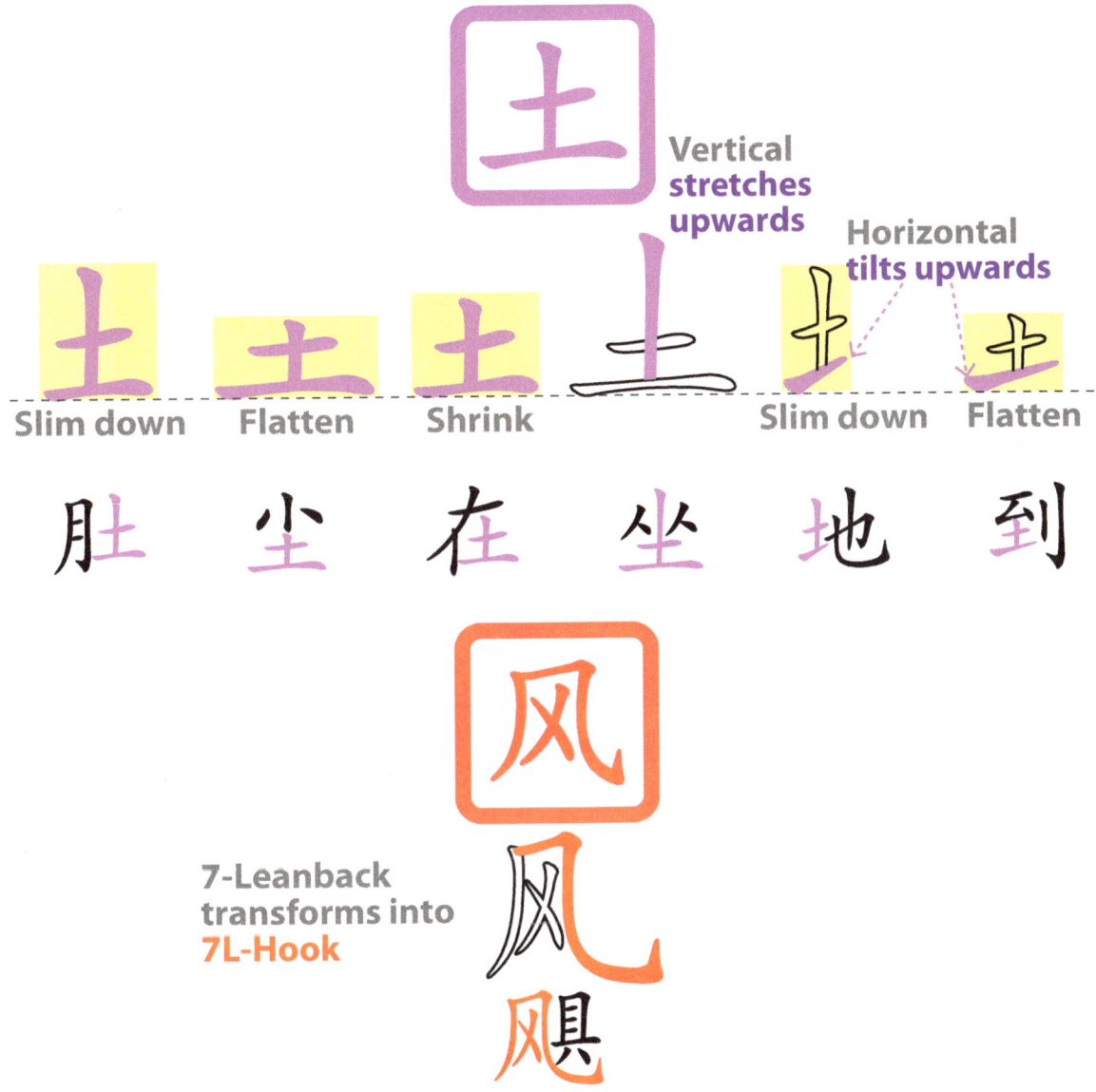

土

Vertical stretches upwards

Horizontal tilts upwards

土 土 土 士 土 土

Slim down **Flatten** **Shrink** **Slim down** **Flatten**

肚 尘 在 坐 地 到

风

7-Leanback transforms into 7L-Hook

风

颶

Activity 23   Stroke Adaptation 1

For each pair of characters, select the type of stroke adaptation (a) to (d) that has taken place and write the alphabet in the bracket.

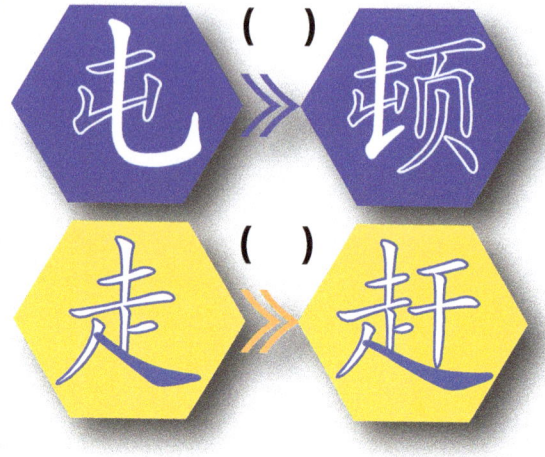

a) Shorten Stroke
b) Stretch Horizontally
c) Horizontal to Tick
d) L-Hook to Vertical Right Hook

Activity 24

For each pair of characters, select the type of stroke adaptation (a) to (f) that has taken place and write the alphabet in the bracket.

女 ( ) 好
是 ( ) 匙

工 ( ) 项
风 ( ) 炮

a) **Shorten Stroke**
b) **Stretch Horizontally**
c) **Horizontal to Tick**
d) **7L-Hook to 7-Back kick**
e) **7-Leanback to 7L-Hook**
f) **7L-Hook to 7-Leanback**

九 ( ) 抛
丸 ( ) 孰

尺 ( ) 咫
秃 ( ) 颓
( )

Types of Stroke Adaptation

1) Horizontally Stretched

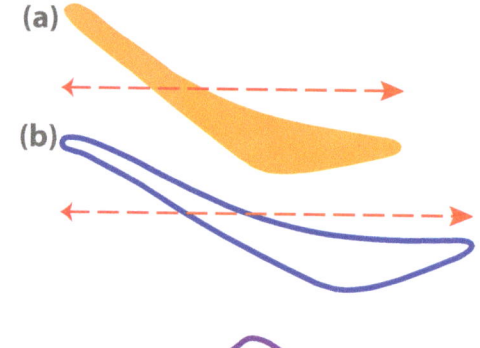

(a)

(b)

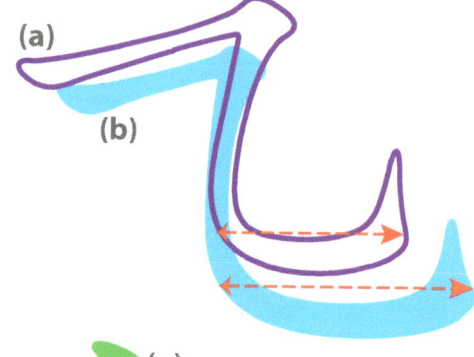

(a)

(b)

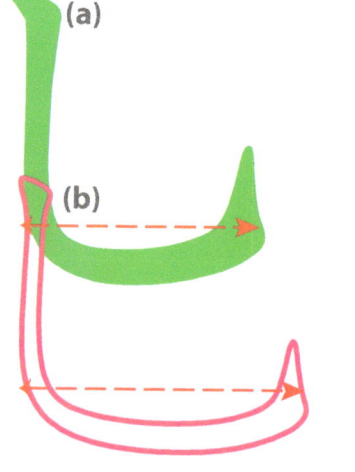

(a)

(b)

2) Stroke Shortened

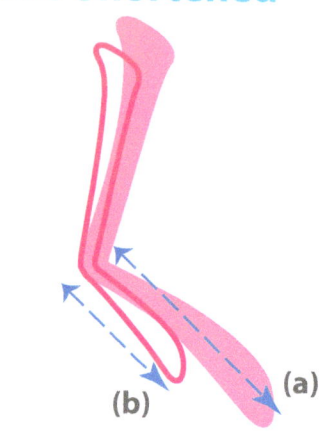

(a)

(b)

3) Angle to Horizontal Changed

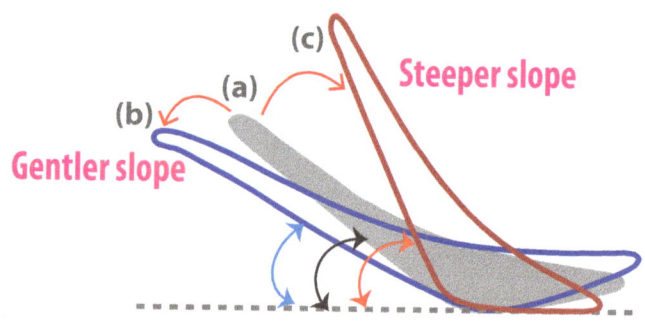

(c)

(a)

(b)

Steeper slope

Gentler slope

Discover the fourth type of stroke adaptation by doing the activity on the next page.

Activity 25
Stroke Adaptation Summary

4) Transformation to a different stroke

Summarise what you have learnt so far. Draw and write the name of the transformed stroke. Go back to Activities 23 and 24 for clues.

1. LR-Slash becomes _____

3. 7-Leanback becomes _____

2a. 7L-Hook becomes **7-Leanback**

4. Horizontal becomes _____

2b. 7L-Hook becomes _____

5. L-Hook becomes _____

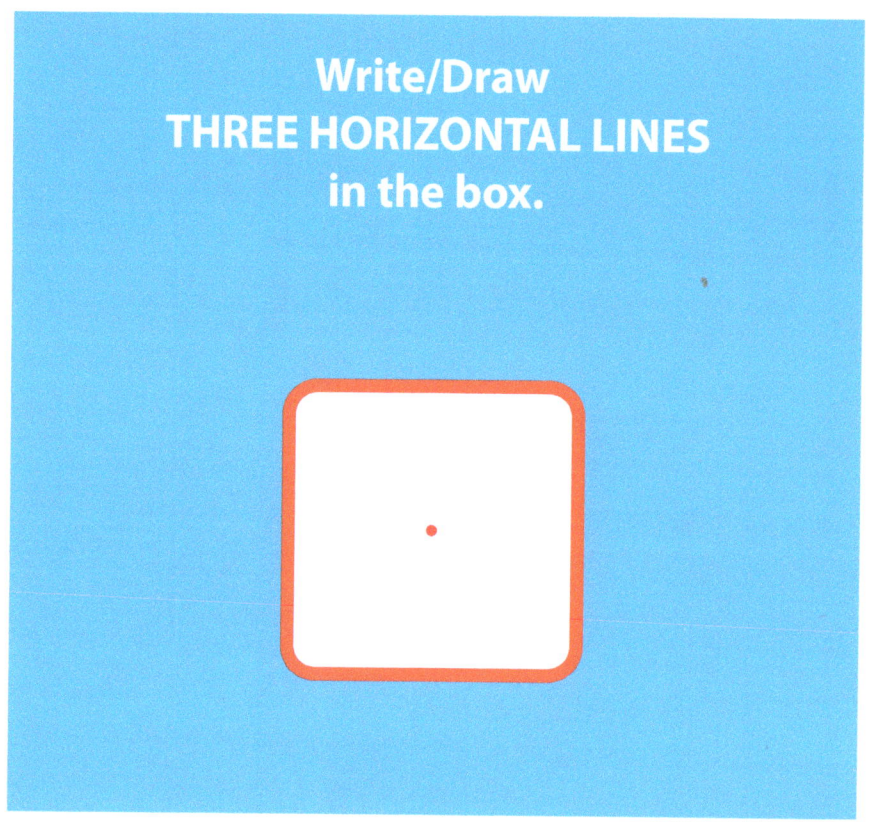

Write/Draw
THREE HORIZONTAL LINES
in the box.

Balance

Balanced is Beautiful

A balanced composition feels right, stable and aesthetically pleasing.

Balance

To create a formation (character) that is stable and aesthetically pleasing, there should be symmetry of parts and alignment of strokes to the imaginery lines.

Symmetry

1. Symmetrical Characters
2. Mostly Symmetrical Characters
3. Non-Symmetrical Characters

Activity 26   Symmetry: English Alphabets

Draw the line of symmetry for these English alphabets such that one side is the mirror image of the other side. See examples shown. Please note that some alphabets have more than one line of symmetry.

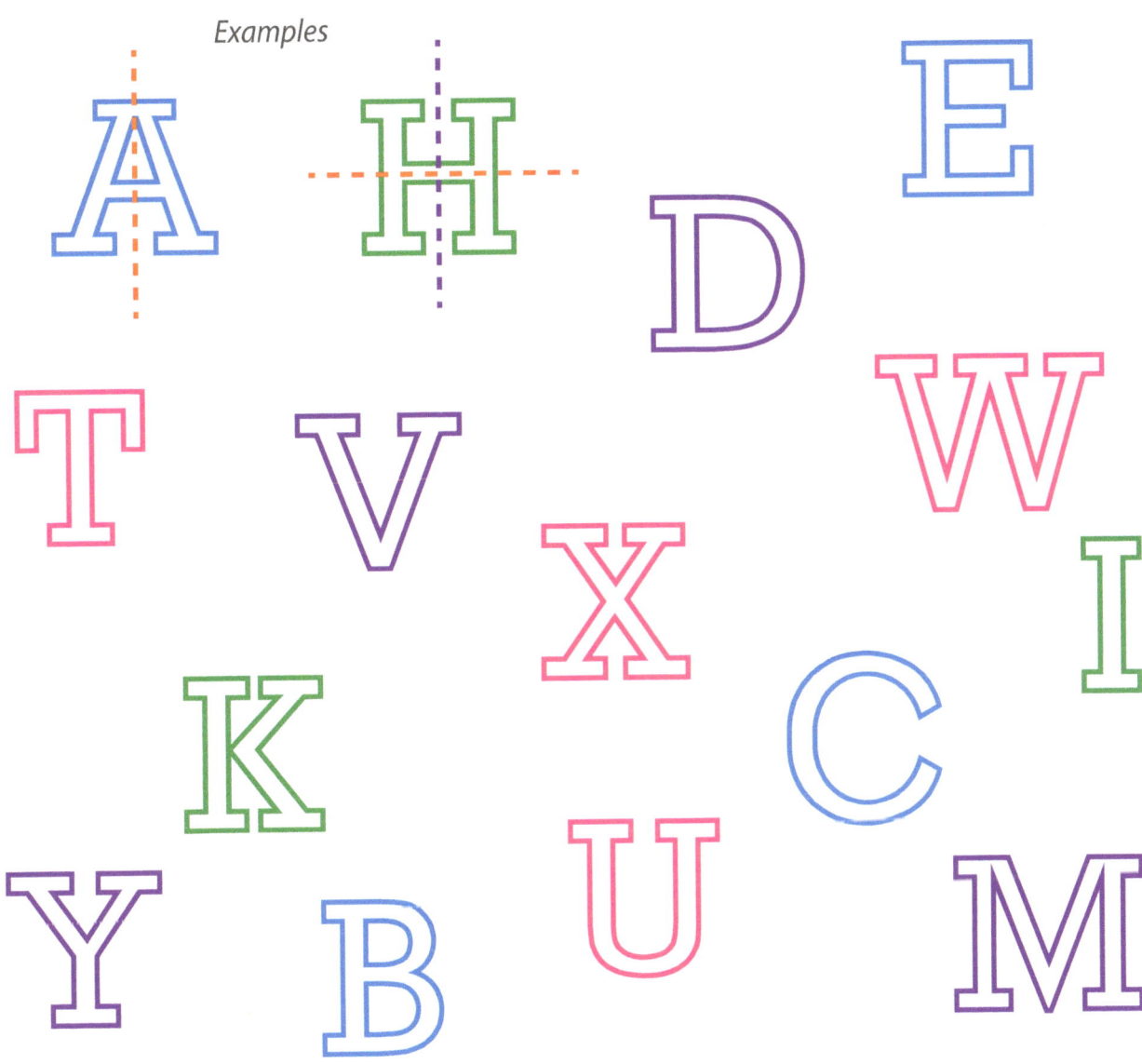

Examples

Symmetry

English alphabets

English alphabets in the previous activity have **bilateral symmetry** or **reflection symmetry**. The **line of symmetry** is usually the horizontal or vertical line that divides the letter into top and bottom or left and right symmetrically—one side is the mirror image of the other side.

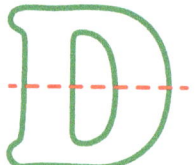 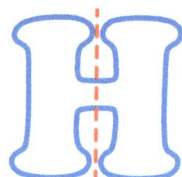

Chinese Characters

If **Chinese characters** are classified according to their appearance, there are basically three types of classification:

a) Symmetrical   **b) Mostly Symmetrical**   **c) Non-Symmetrical**

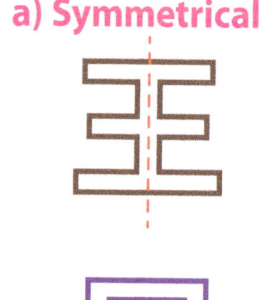      

If the characters are **symmetrical** or **mostly symmetrical**, make sure that the symmetrical parts are balanced when writing.

Balanced

All the three types of characters (symmetrical, mostly symmetrical and non-symmetrical) are shown here. Observe how they are created to look balanced.

a) Left Side and Right Side

Compare the **first two characters** of each row. Observe how the strokes on the left side and right side of each character are positioned. Which character looks balanced? Which looks unbalanced? Why?

c) Angle to the Horizontal

Dots, Tick and Slashes are slanted at an angle to the horizontal.
Observe how changes in these angles change the look of the character.

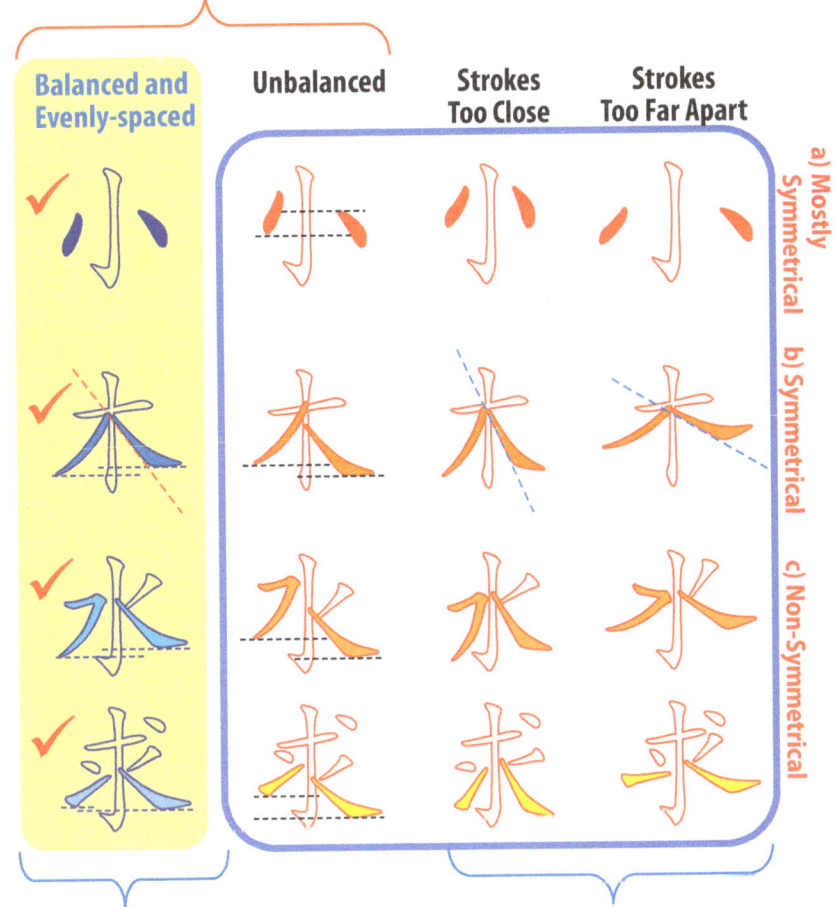

b) Distance from the middle stroke(s)

Compare the **last two characters** with the **first character.** How far or close should the strokes on the two sides be positioned from the middle?

Activity 27
Symmetrical Characters 1

Draw the symmetrical part(s).
Use the imaginery lines
(dotted lines) to guide you in
your drawing.

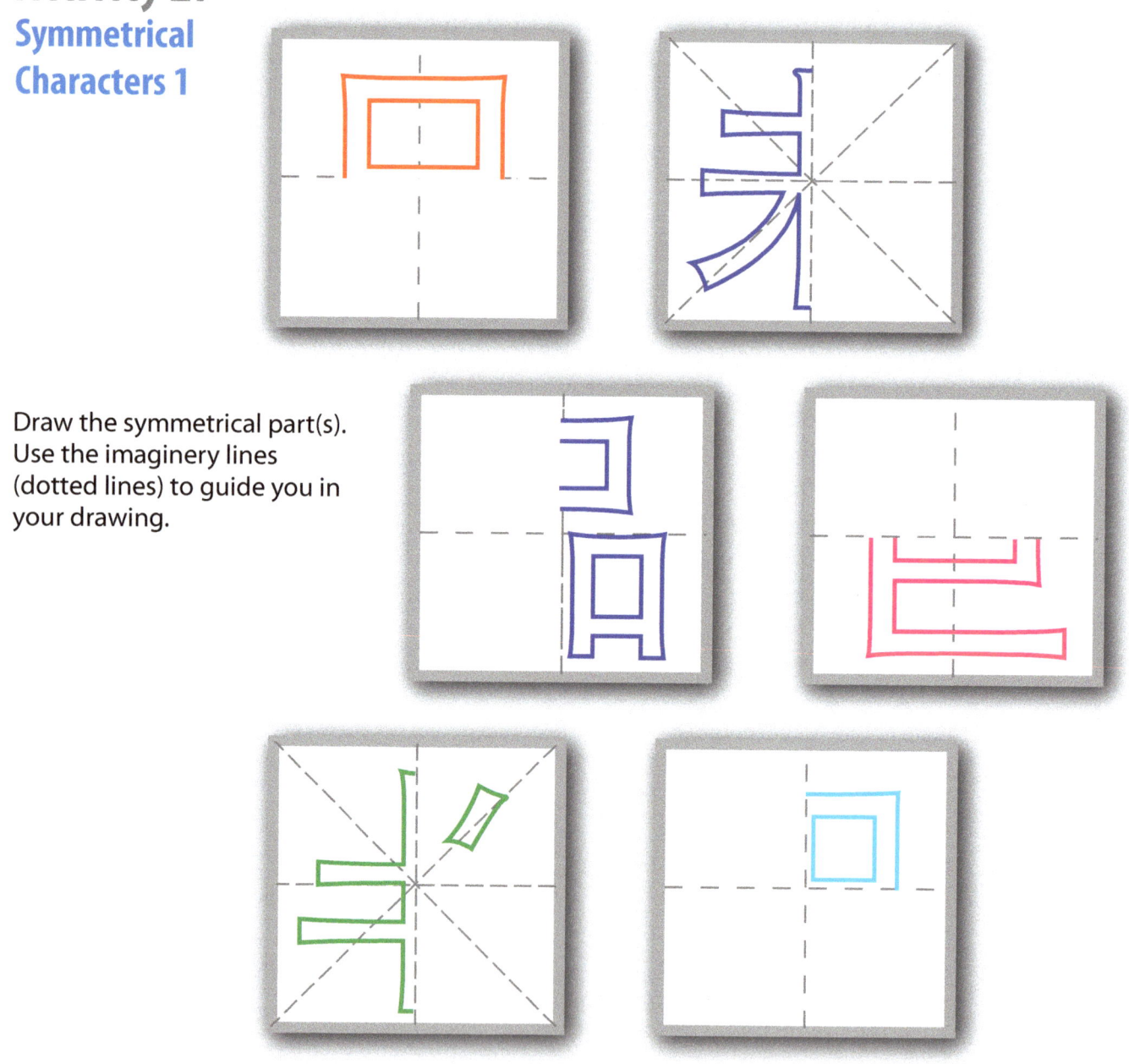

Draw the symmetrical part(s).

Activity 28
Symmetrical Characters 2

Shade the boxes symmetrically along the red line. See example.

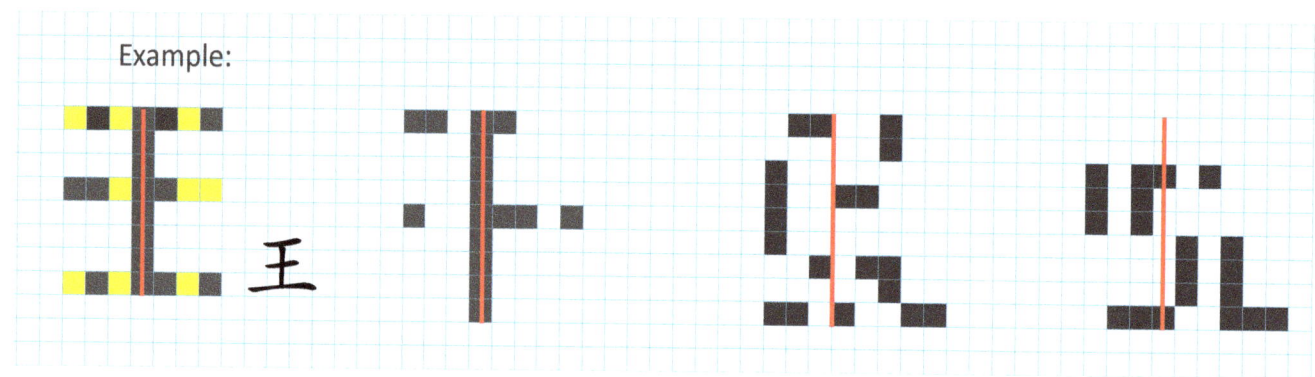

Example:

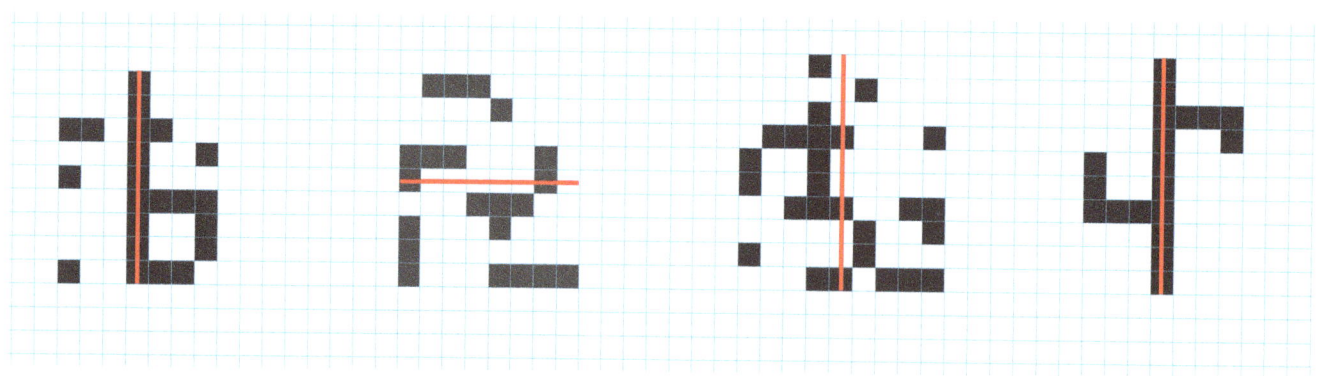

More activities on 'Symmetry' on the last few pages. Try them out.

Activity 29
'Mostly-Symmetrical' Characters

These characters are mostly symmetrical.
a) **Draw** the line of symmetry and
b) **Circle** the part(s) that is/are not symmetrical. See example.

Example:

再 井 面 杀 言 事 百 乘 乘 雨 害 盒 重 童 全 金 常 变

Spacing Between Strokes

The following tips are general rules that can be applied to any type of characters. The shaded boxes and dotted lines show the spaces between strokes. Observe how the strokes are evenly-spaced to make the characters look balanced.

a) Evenly-spaced Strokes

b) Vertical Spacing

c) Horizontal Spacing

d) Vertical and Horizontal Spacing

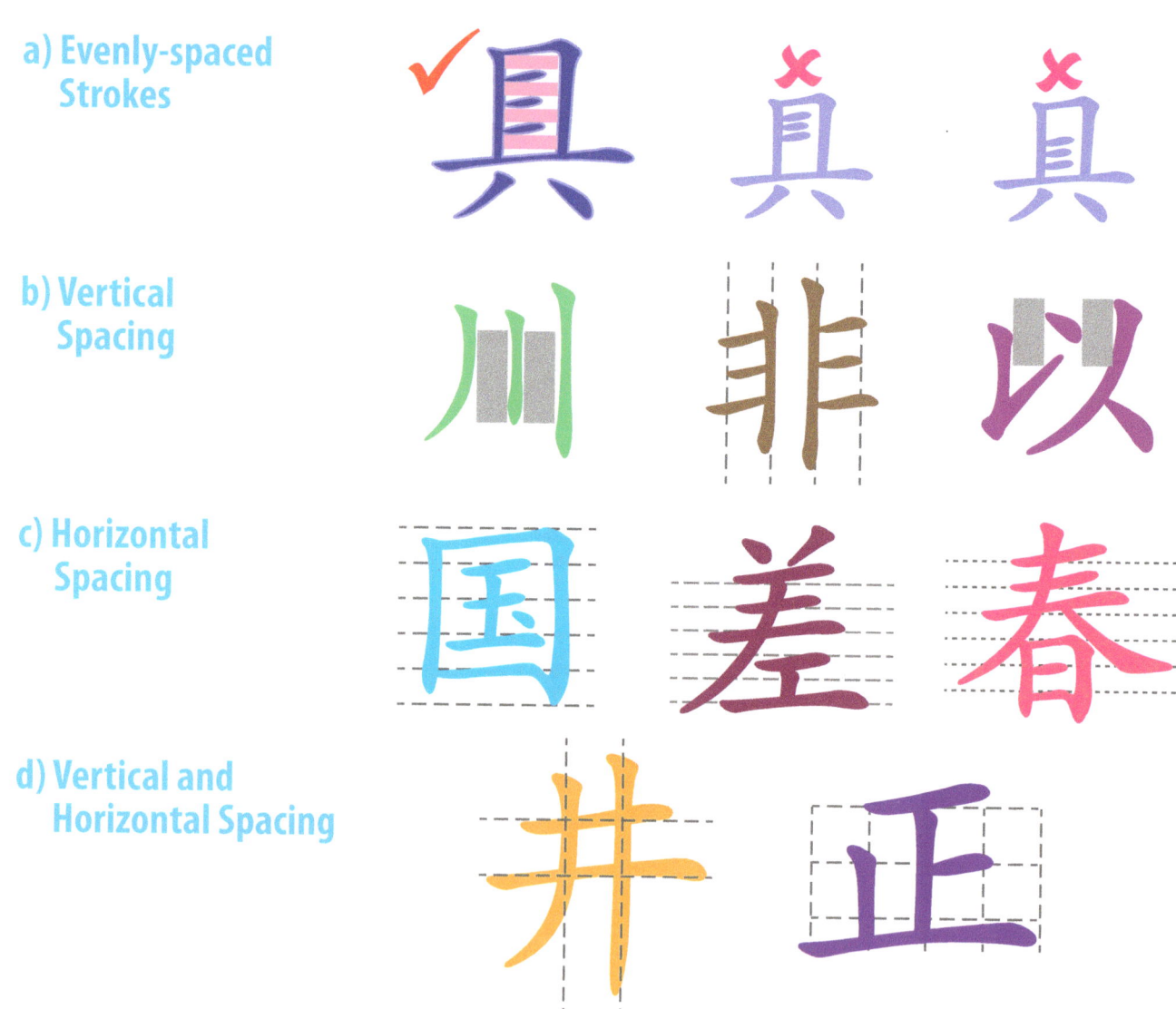

Diagonals and Spacing

Diagonals are good reference points for **Slashes and Curls**.
Observe how these strokes align to the diagonals.
Observe the spaces between the strokes and if these strokes are also parallel to one another.

e) Spacing Between Slashes

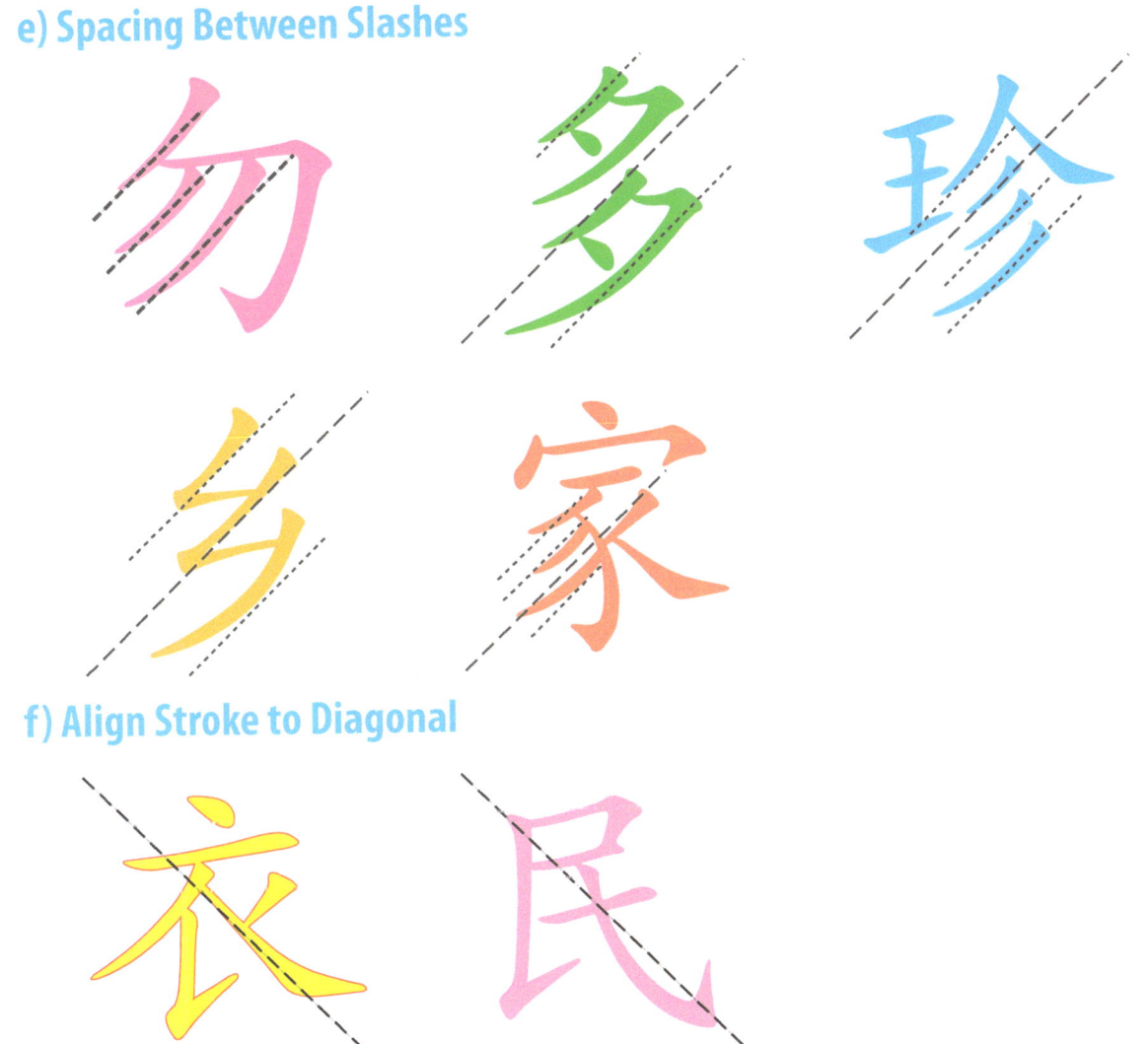

f) Align Stroke to Diagonal

More Unspoken Rules

1. Midpoint

Take note of the positioning of this part in the character.

2. Longer bottom

Note that when the same stroke or part is repeated in the same character, the bottom stroke/part is usually longer. There are some exceptions. *(See page 145 for an exception to this rule)*

3. Parallel

Note how the strokes slanting in the same direction are aligned to be parallel to one another.

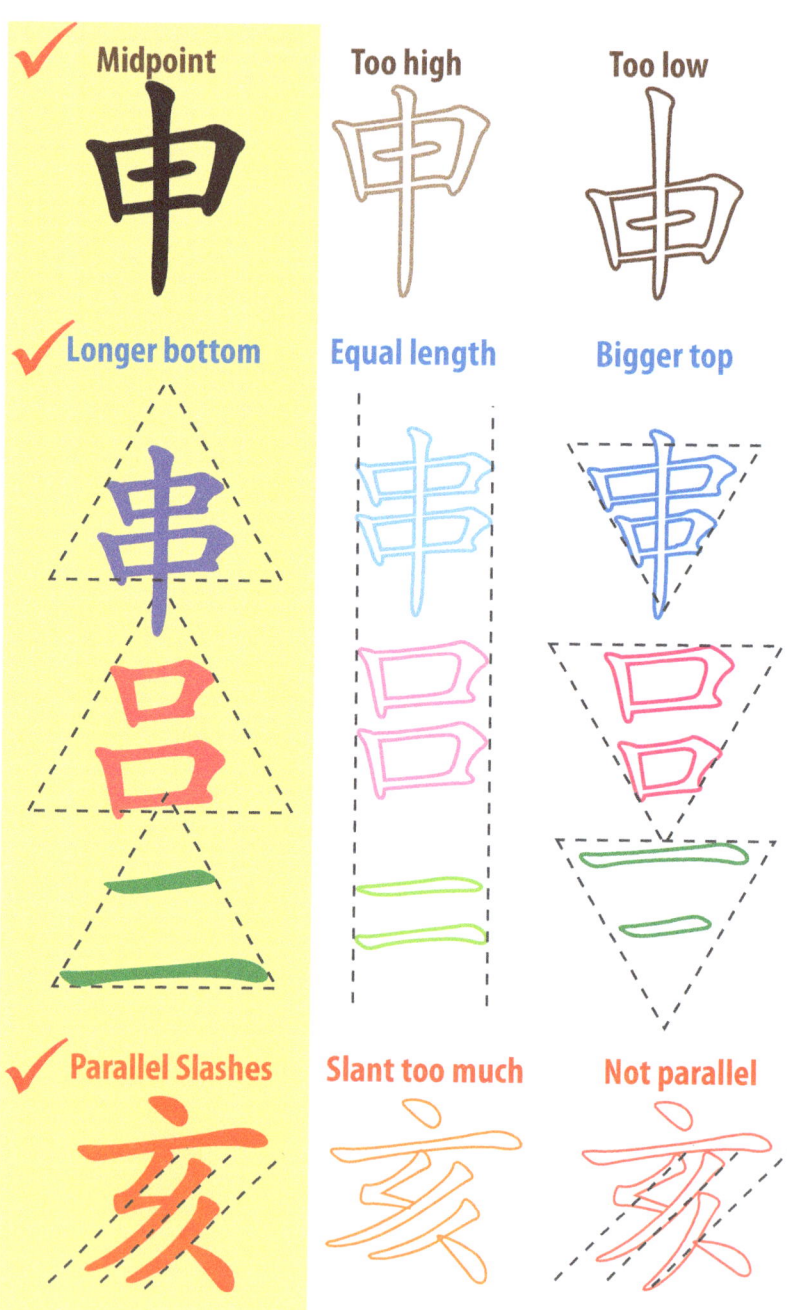

✓ Midpoint　　Too high　　Too low

✓ Longer bottom　　Equal length　　Bigger top

✓ Parallel Slashes　　Slant too much　　Not parallel

Centre

The centre of the box stage is the most important reference point for the performers (strokes) to ensure that the formation (character) look balanced and centred.

Circle

1. Circle of Equal Distance
2. Imaginery Circles
3. Centre of Character

Shape

1. Shape of Character

Circle of Equal Distance

Other than the imaginery straight lines mentioned in 'Basic Structures', there is also an **imaginary circle** within the square. Note that a character is usually kept within this circle and none of its strokes touches the box.

The centre is a very important reference point for the positioning of strokes.

The distance from the centre of a circle to any part of the circumference (outline) of the circle is always equal. This distance is called the radius.

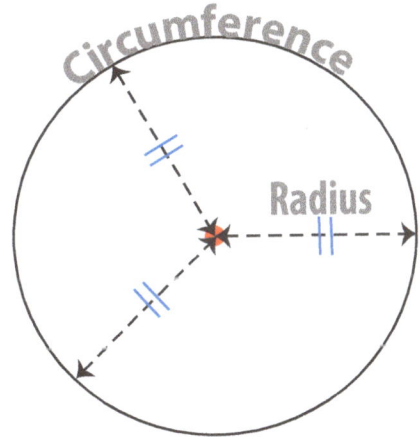

Imaginery Circle

Positioning of Strokes

The imaginery circle(s) help you to position the strokes more precisely.

a) Vertical protrudes inner circle

c) Dots and Horizontal are within the inner circle

d) Vertical and Slashes are within the outer circle.

b) Slashes protrude inner circle

If any of the stroke juts out from the circle (as shown), the character will not look balanced and centred.

Stretch Points

Stretch Point (SP) is a point on an imaginery circle where a stroke aims to reach out to. The stroke can be

- **a) Near to the SP but does not touch it,**
- **b) Touches the SP or**
- **c) Stretches slightly beyond it.**

Analysing the possible Stretch Points that a character possesses will show how a character 'centres' itself in the square box so that it looks balanced.

Single Circle

A) Go back to page 96. How did you write the character? Draw a circle around the character to discover where are the Stretch Points? Compare with this writing.

This is a very simple character with only one stroke. The 3-Stretch Point way of writing gives the character a heavy base and light top.

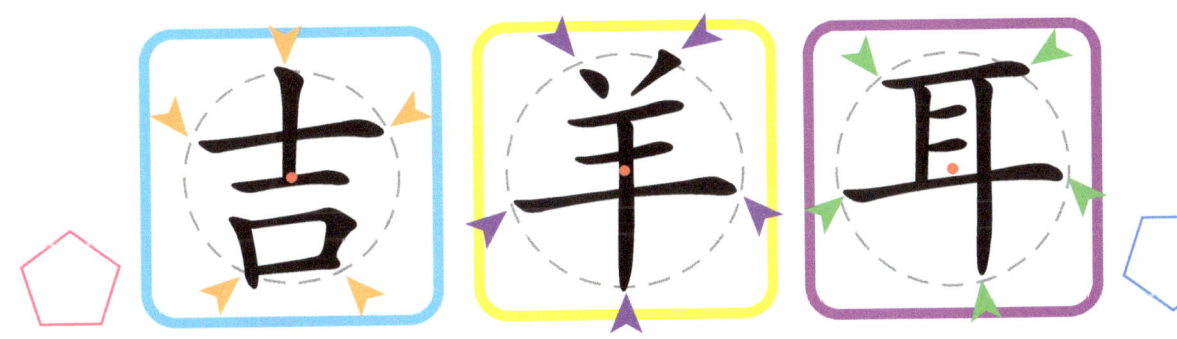

B) Observe how these three characters fit nicely into a circle with five Stretch Points. Join these five points within each character. Do you get a 5-sided polygon?

Notice the first two characters are Symmetrical, the third character is 'Mostly Symmetrical'?

Two Concentric Circles

A) These two characters are written with the same imaginery circles. Flip one character upside down, you will discover that the part 'T' —formed by a vertical and a horizontal—are identical in both characters.

Coincidentally, these two characters have opposite meaning—the character on the left means **'UP'** and the one on the right means **'DOWN'.**

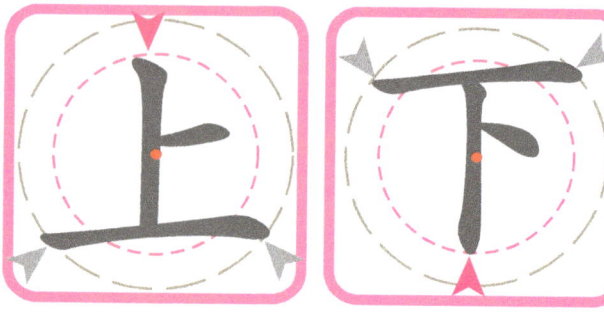

B) Focus on the Stretch Points on the inner and outer circles. Observe how the characters are centred.

Concentric circles are circles overlapping one another and sharing the same centre.

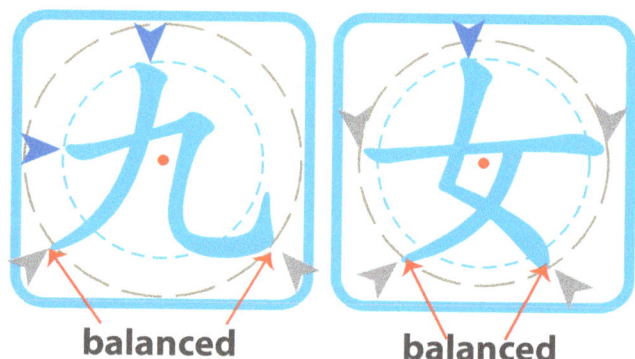

balanced   **balanced**

C) This character is more complicated. Observe how it is centred. First look at the five Stretch Points on the outer circle. Then zoom in on the five Stretch Points on the inner circle.

5 Stretch Points

Three Concentric Circles

These two characters are non-symmetrical. Observe how the strokes stretch to different circles and still maintain its LR and TB balance.

Balanced on the left and right sides (LR Balance)

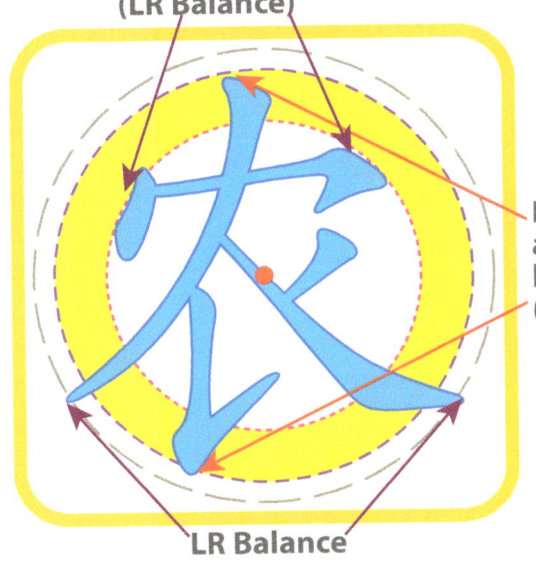

Balanced at the top and bottom (TB Balance)

LR Balance

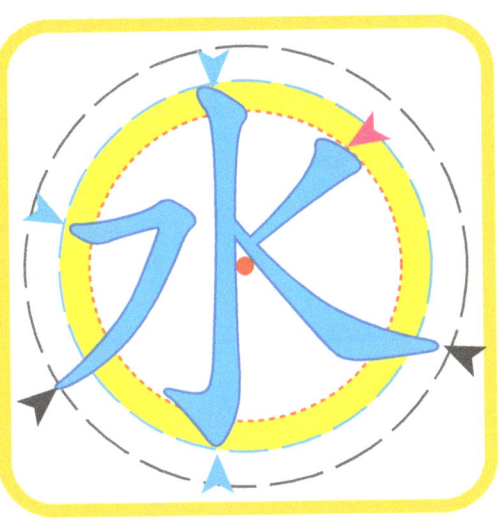

Four Concentric Circles

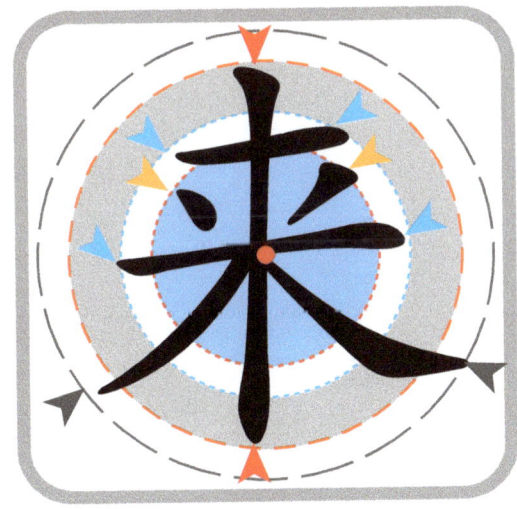

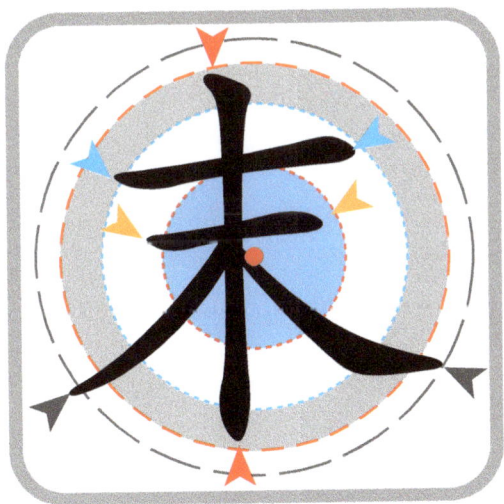

Activity 30
Imaginery Circles

Draw circle(s) in the boxes (as shown in previous pages) to determine the Stretch Points. The red dot is the centre.
For more accurate drawings, use a compass. Read Section 4 on how to draw circles with a compass.

Draw 1 to 2 circles

Draw 3 circles

Draw 4 circles

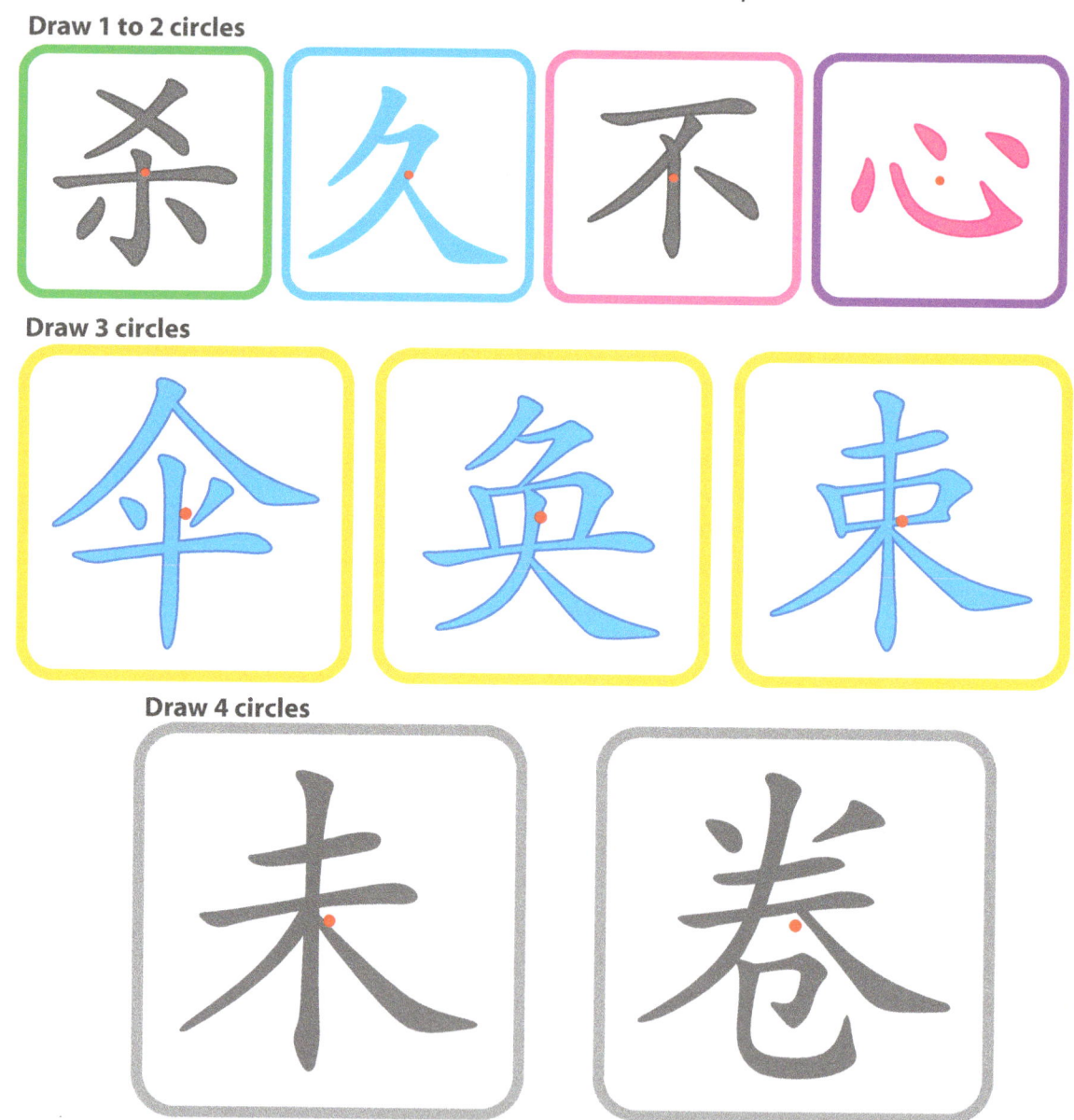

Centre of Character

Writing in a line

Another use of the centre of circle is to help you gauge the centre of character. Having some sense of the centre of character helps you to align characters in a line and space them out evenly when writing them by hand.

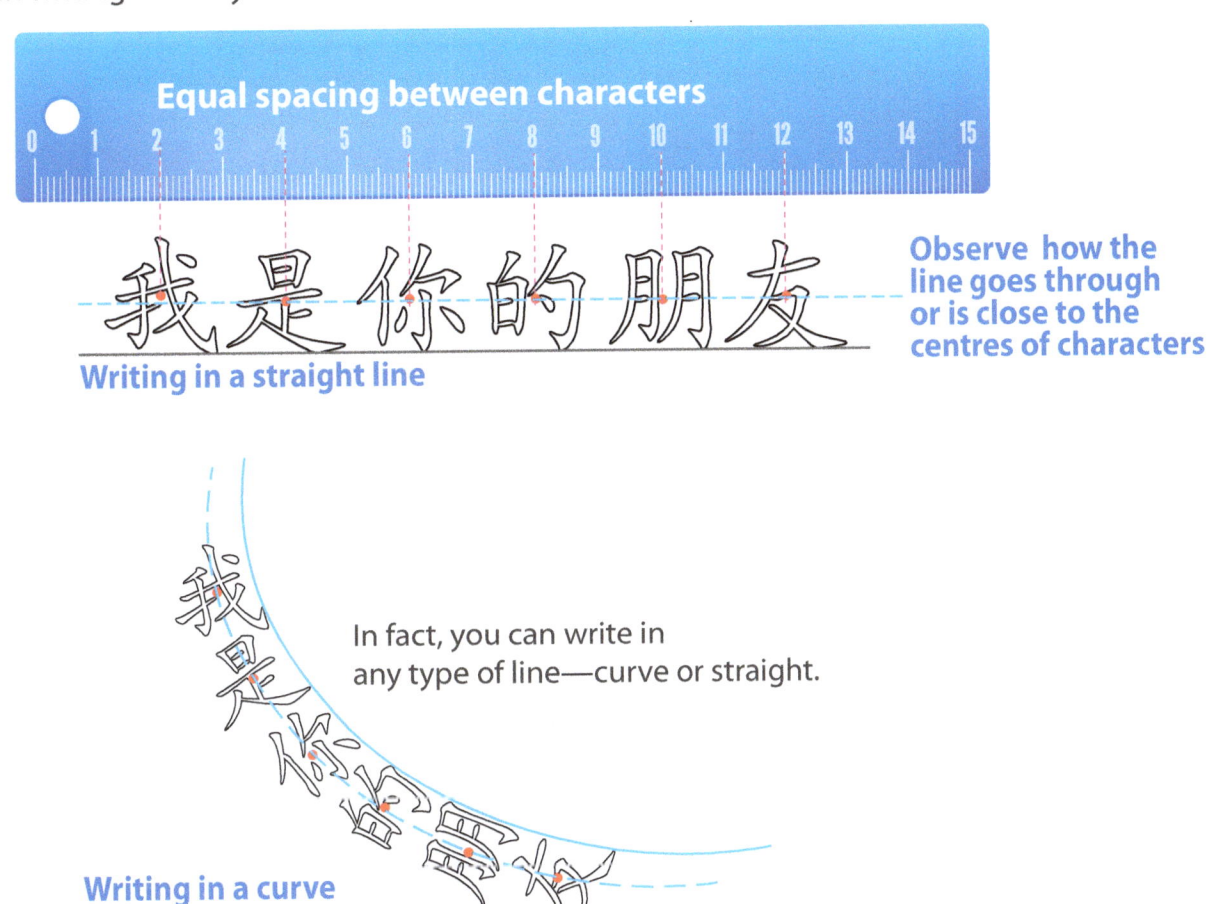

Equal spacing between characters

Writing in a straight line

Observe how the line goes through or is close to the centres of characters

In fact, you can write in any type of line—curve or straight.

Writing in a curve

With practice, you will be able to write characters with or without the lines.

Activity 31   Centre of Character

Indicate the centre of the character with a red dot. Note the red dot may fall on the strokes or any space inside the character. See examples. Use any tool that can help you.

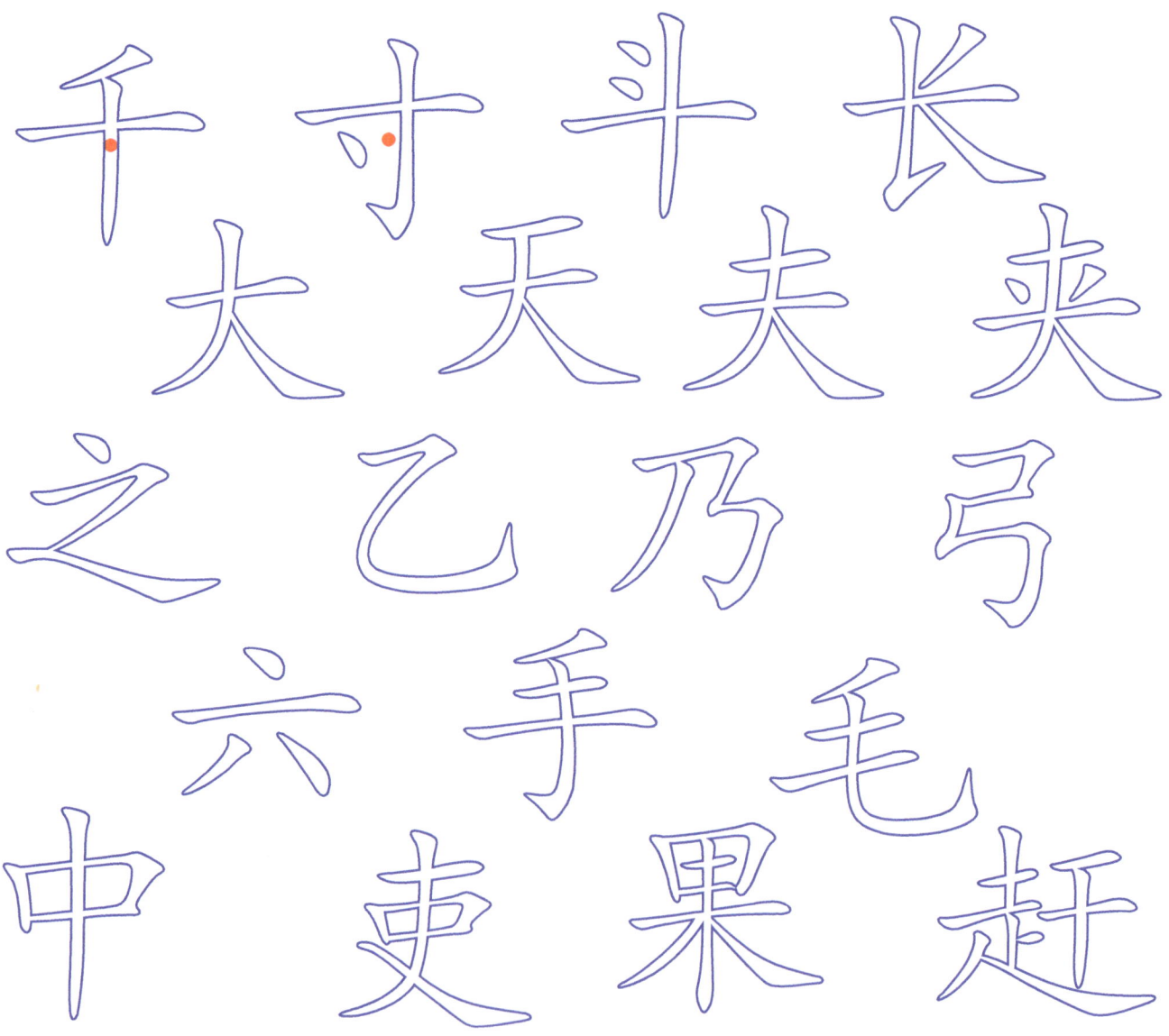

Singapore

Each character has a different silhouette, that is if you blur out the strokes and just look at its outline, you can see that the character fits into a common shape such as a triangle, rectangle or trapezium. They can also fit into other multi-sided polygons like pentagon, hexagon and heptagon.

Note: A polygon is a two-dimensional shape formed by straight lines.

Shapes of Alphabets

Do you think an English alphabet has a shape? Observe how these alphabets fit into common shapes such as triangle, rectangle and oval.

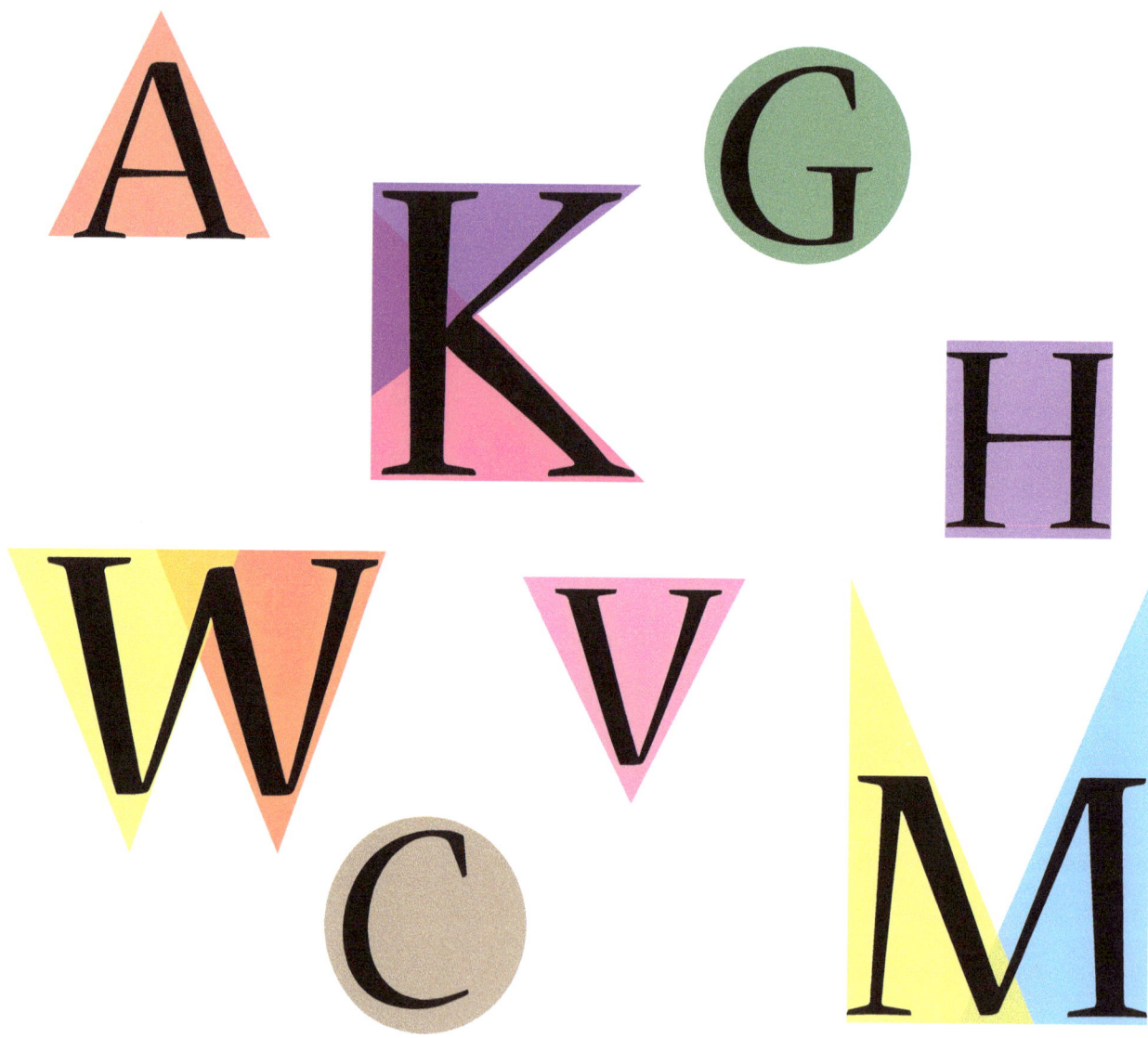

Refer to what you have written/drawn on page 118. Which of the following is closer to your writing/drawing?

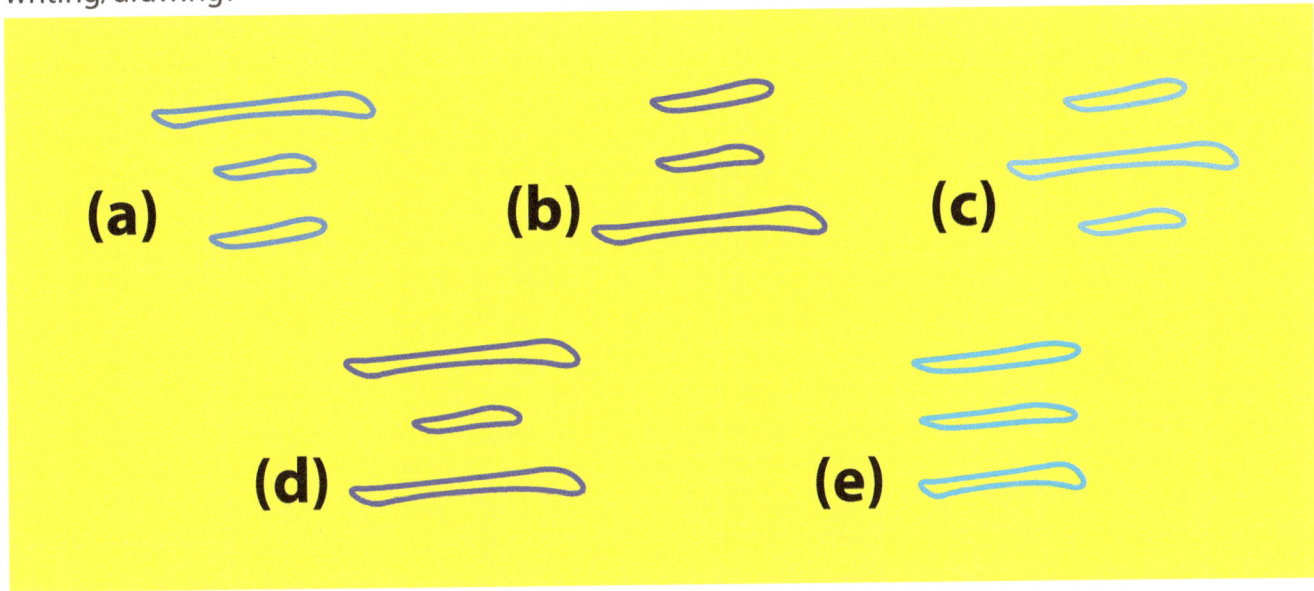

Did you write the three horizontal lines with equal lengths or unequal lengths? If they are unequal, which horizontal is the longest? Which is the shortest?

For those who have not learnt Chinese, you probably do not see any difference in these variations. However, a native Chinese will only recognise **option (b)** as the Chinese character for number '3'.

Many beginners are not sensitive to differences in the relative lengths of strokes so using 'shapes' will help them to notice such differences.

Relative Lengths and Shape

Longer Bottom Horizontal

Observe how the look of these three characters change when the horizontals are written in equal lengths or with a longer upper horizontal. Notice in the second row, the character is transformed into another character when the upper horizontal is longer than the lower horizontal.

This character has a different meaning from the first character

On the next page, notice the characters In the last row have longer **middle** horizontal. On the page after, there is a character with a longer **top** horizontal. Observe how their shapes are different.

Body Shape of Character

Observe how these Chinese characters fit into these shapes.

1) Triangle (3-sided)

2) Trapezium (4-sided)

3) Rectangle (4-sided)

4) Pentagon (5-sided)

5) Hexagon (6-sided)

6) Heptagon (7-sided)

Why Body Shape?

Shapes are easily understood by learners from any language background. Learners can visualise shapes easily.

Body shapes of characters bring attention to the:

a) Relative Lengths of its Width and Height

These three characters vary in shape due to differences between their widths and heights.

The first character has a longer width than height; the second character has a longer height than width and the last character has the same width and height.

b) Relative Lengths of Strokes

Both characters have three horizontal lines. Their body shapes change due to the difference in their lengths. One has the longest bottom horizontal and the other has the longest top horizontal.

c) Position of a Part

The shape of the character changes when the rectangular part is placed nearer to the top than to the bottom.

Determine Body Shape

Table on the next page:
The table shows the common shapes that some characters have.

How to Determine the Body Shape of a Character:

1. Zoom in on the Top & Base
of a character and observe if it is **pointed or flat**. Then pick one of the four types listed in the left column of the table.

2. Choose a sub-category
by observing which part (top, middle or base) of the character is the broadest or if all the parts are of the same width.

3. Adjust the corners
of the shape to fit the character.

NOTE: Not all the characters will fit into these common shapes. Start from simple characters with fewer strokes.

Common Shapes of Characters

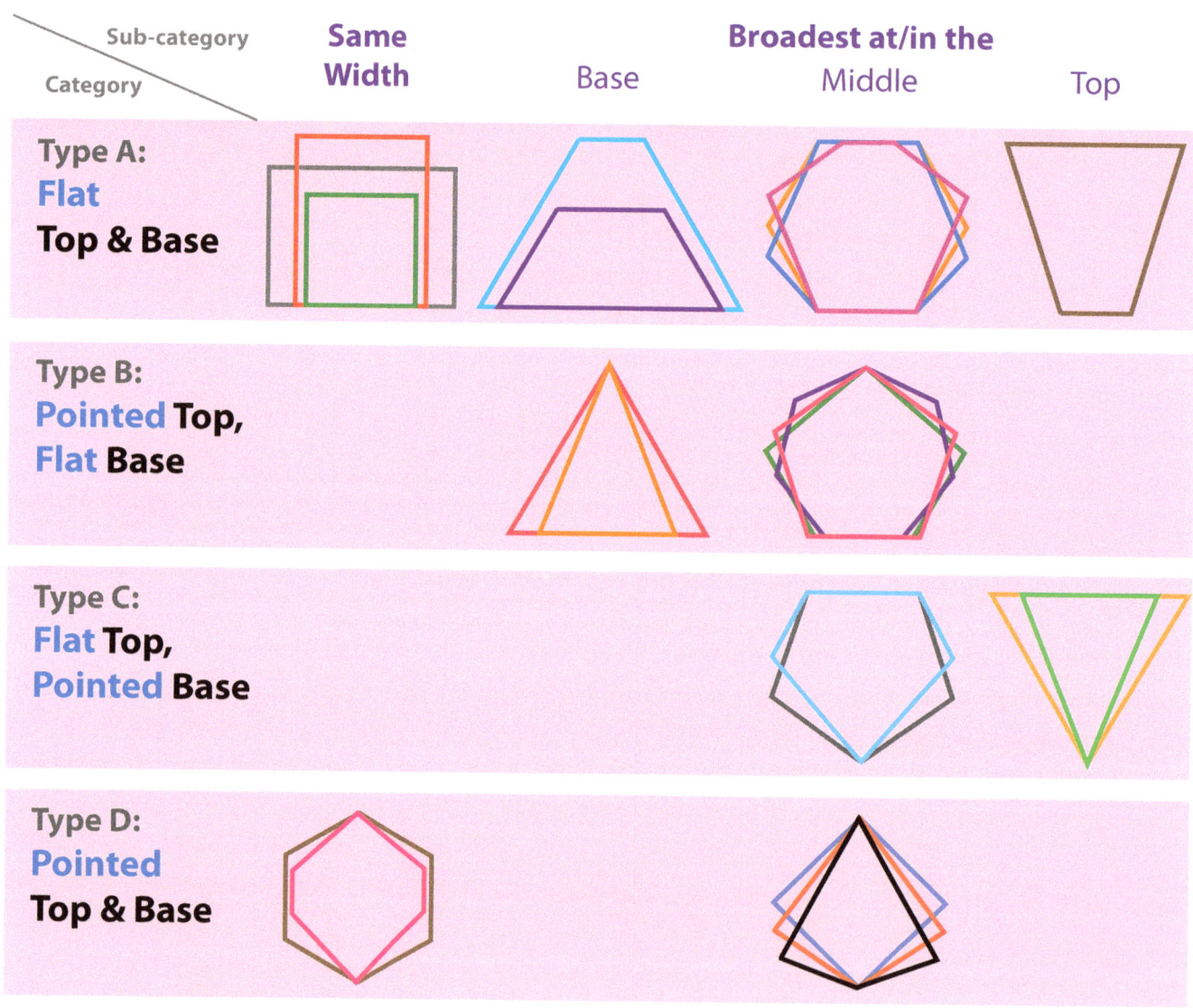

	Sub-category	**Same Width**	**Broadest at/in the**		
Category			Base	Middle	Top
Type A: **Flat** **Top & Base**					
Type B: **Pointed** Top, **Flat** Base					
Type C: **Flat** Top, **Pointed** Base					
Type D: **Pointed** **Top & Base**					

Activity 32
Body Shape of Character

Use the method described in the previous pages to determine the body shapes of the characters. Write the alphabets in the brackets. Note the shape can be used more than once.

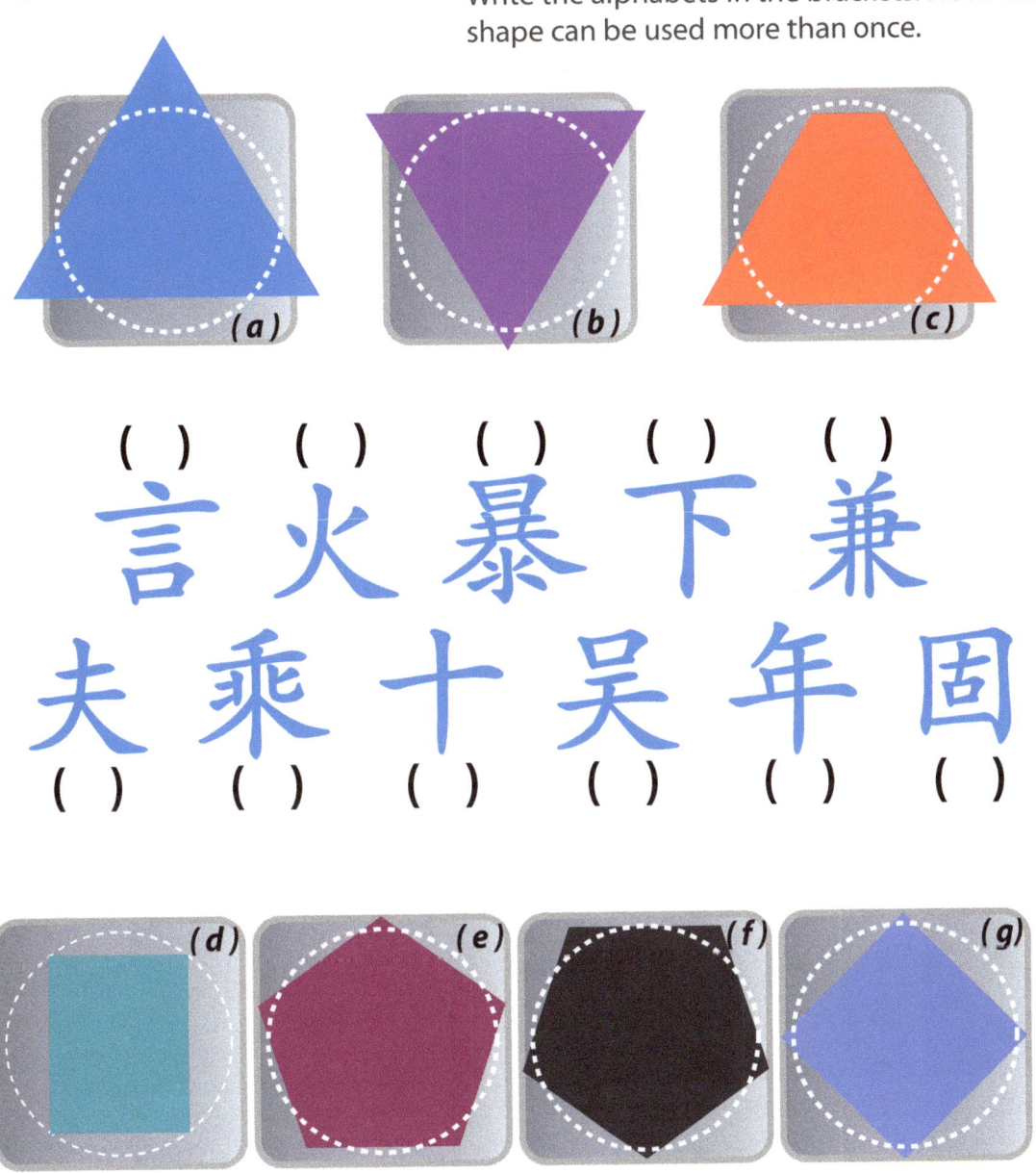

(a) (b) (c)

( ) ( ) ( ) ( ) ( )

言 火 暴 下 兼

夫 乘 十 吴 年 固

( ) ( ) ( ) ( ) ( ) ( )

(d) (e) (f) (g)

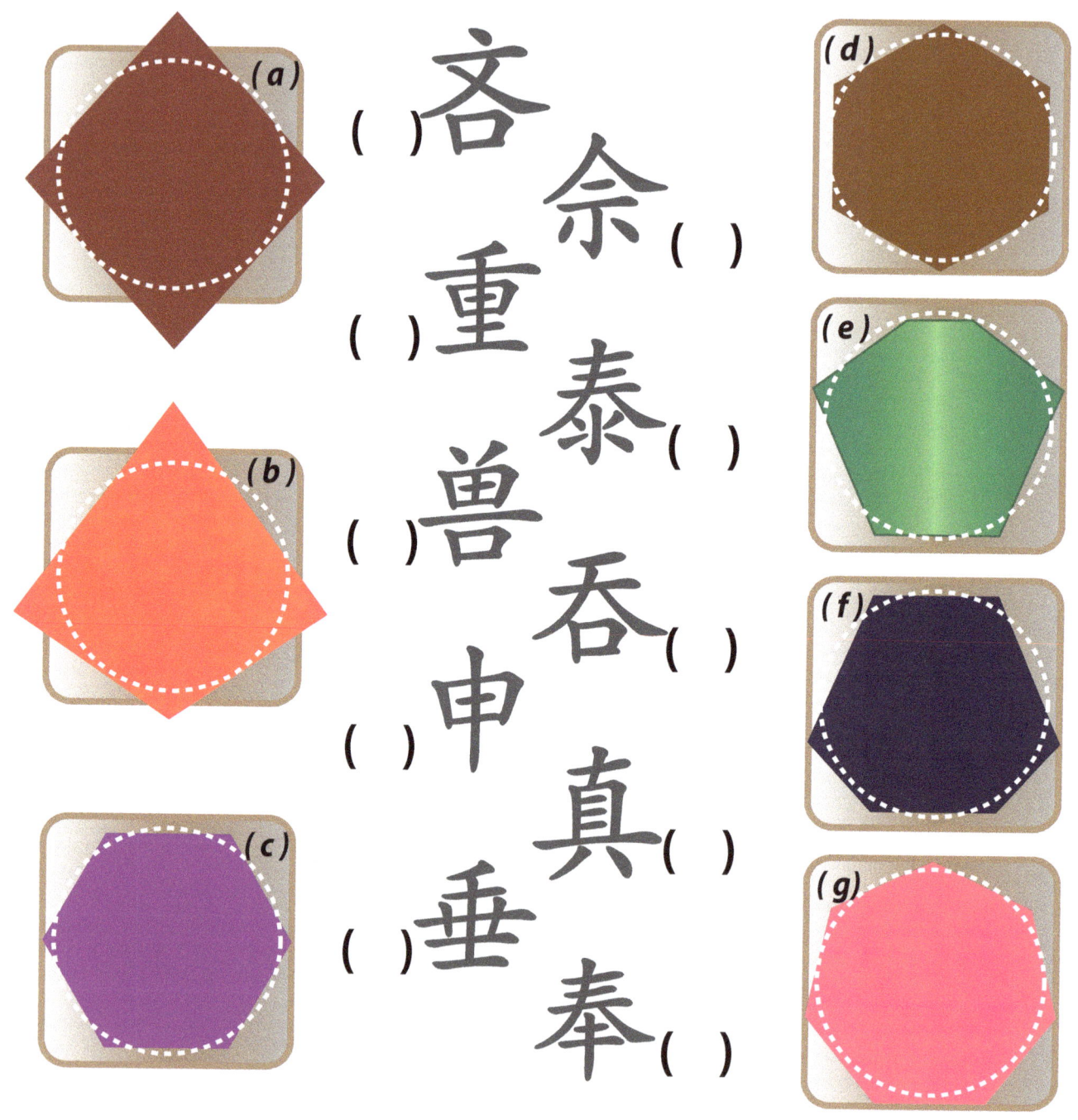

( ) 㑪
( ) 重
( ) 兽
( ) 申
佘 ( )
泰 ( )
吞 ( )
真 ( )
垂
奉 ( )

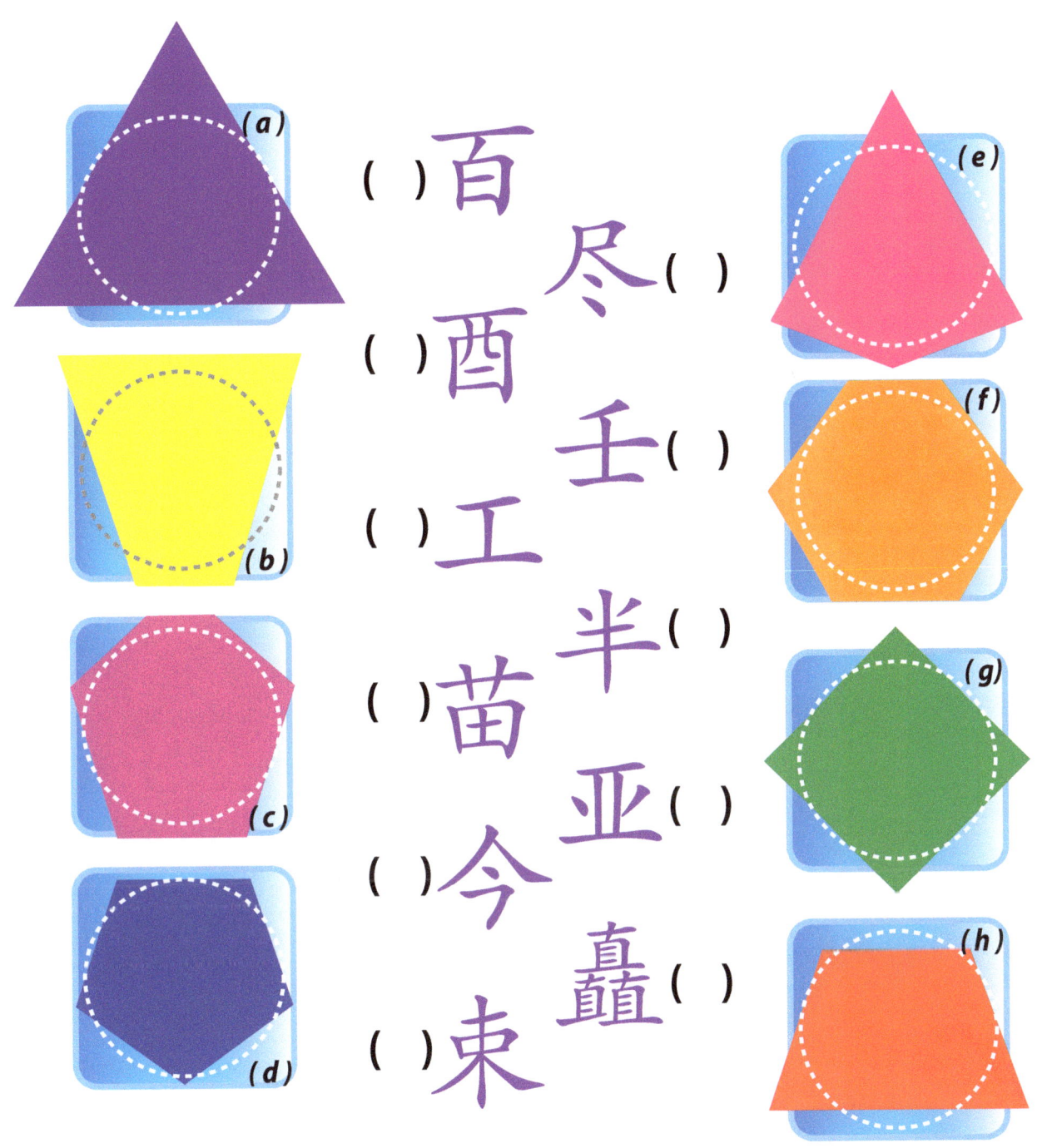

( ) 百
( ) 酉
( ) 工
( ) 苗
( ) 今
( ) 束

( ) 尽
( ) 壬
( ) 半
( ) 亚
( ) 蟲

Activity 33
Spot the Differences 1

Develop your ability to distinguish between twinlike characters. Spot the difference(s) in each pair of characters and colour the difference(s) in the **outlined** character. See example.

1. 万 方

2. 刀 刃

3. 习 习

4. 予 矛

5. 勿 匆

6. 同 同

7. 印 印

8. 氏 氐

9. 巾 帀

10. 九 丸

11. 几 凡

12. 艮 良

13. 戈 戋

14. 戎 戒

15. 冉 再

Develop your ability to distinguish between twinlike characters. Spot the difference(s) in each pair of characters and colour the difference(s) in the **outlined** character.

16. 乌 鸟

17. 厂 广

18. 卜 下

19. 十 千

20. 干 午

21. 斤 斥

22. 士 壬

23. 夫 失

24. 未 朱

25. 夕 歹

26. 古 舌

27. 又 叉

28. 史 吏

29. 今 令

30. 兰 羊

Develop your ability to distinguish between twinlike characters. Spot the difference(s) in each pair of characters and colour the difference(s) in the **outlined** character.

31. 从 丛

32. 不 丕

33. 火 灭

34. 皿 血

35. 目 自

36. 旦 亘

37. 勺 匀

38. 日 旧

39. 三 丰

40. 米 来

41. 立 产

42. 其 甚

43. 帅 师

44. 代 伐

45. 李 季

Develop your ability to distinguish between twinlike characters. Spot the difference(s) in each pair of characters and colour the difference(s) in the **outlined** character.

46. 幻 幼

47. 亨 享

48. 茶 荼

49. 汁 汗

50. 坏 环

51. 故 敌

52. 快 快

53. 侯 候

54. 狠 狼

55. 休 体

56. 人 火

57. 天 关

58. 父 交

59. 买 卖

60. 允 充

Develop your ability to distinguish between twinlike characters. Spot the difference(s) in each pair of characters and colour the difference(s) in the **outlined** character.

61. 开 并

62. 卯 卯

63. 卓 桌

64. 用 角

65. 巴 色

66. 丹 舟

67. 逐 遂

68. 元 先

69. 垠 琅

70. 受 爱

71. 束 柬

72. 六 兴

73. 乖 乘

74. 下 卡

75. 栗 粟

Develop your ability to distinguish between twinlike characters. Spot the difference(s) in each pair of characters and colour the difference(s) in the **outlined** character.

76. 买 实
77. 尺 尽
78. 巨 臣
79. 中 虫
80. 幺 玄

81. 全 金
82. 工 左
83. 山 击
84. 水 丞
85. 且 县

86. 直 真
87. 具 真
88. 盅 盉
89. 壁 璧
90. 吕 昌

Activity 34
Spot the Differences 2

Spot the difference(s) in each pair of characters and colour the difference(s) in **both** character.
See example.

91. 岚 岗

92. 着 眷

93. 亭 亮

94. 爪 瓜

95. 前 俞

96. 衣 农

97. 开 井

98. 星 皇

99. 未 末

100. 东 乐

101. 杖 枚

102. 友 反

103. 伞 平

104. 平 乎

105. 刀 力

Spot the difference(s) in each pair of characters and colour the difference(s) in **both** character.

106. 凤 凤

107. 名 各

108. 庄 压

109. 佘 余

110. 义 叉

111. 午 牛

112. 矢 失

113. 水 永

Activity 35
Spot the Differences 3

Compare the characters in each set. Spot the difference(s) between the outlined characters and the shaded character and colour the differences in the **outlined** characters.

114. 大 天 天

119. 大 太 犬

115. 七 毛 毛

120. 儿 兀 元

116. 云 去 丢

121. 戊 戍 成

117. 王 玉 主

122. 杳 查 香

118. 业 亚 严

123. 哀 衰 衷

124. 力 办 为

125. 兄 兑 克

126. 贝 贞 负

127. 口 石 右

128. 己 己 巳

129. 上 止 正

130. 丘 兵 兵 兵

131. 尸 户 卢 尺

132. 木 本 术 禾

133. 了 子 子 子

134. 田 由 甲 申

Adapt, Balance, Centre

1. Summarise what you have learnt about the third set of ABC (Adapt, Balance and Centre). Feel free to express in your own ways ... use words, illustrations, clippings ...

2. Using the concepts learnt, compare and contrast the composition of **Chinese characters** and **English words** (or any language you know).

   E.g. Where is the centre of an English word?

   E.g. What 'shape' is it?

My Reflection

3. Apply the concepts learnt on the third set of ABC to analyse some of the Chinese Characters in Activities 33-35.

My Questions:

Without turning back to earlier pages, name these strokes with **LEFT HOOK.**

(a) ☐ (b) ☐ (c) ☐ (d) ☐ (e) ☐ (f) ☐

Without turning back to earlier pages, name these strokes with **RIGHT HOOK.**

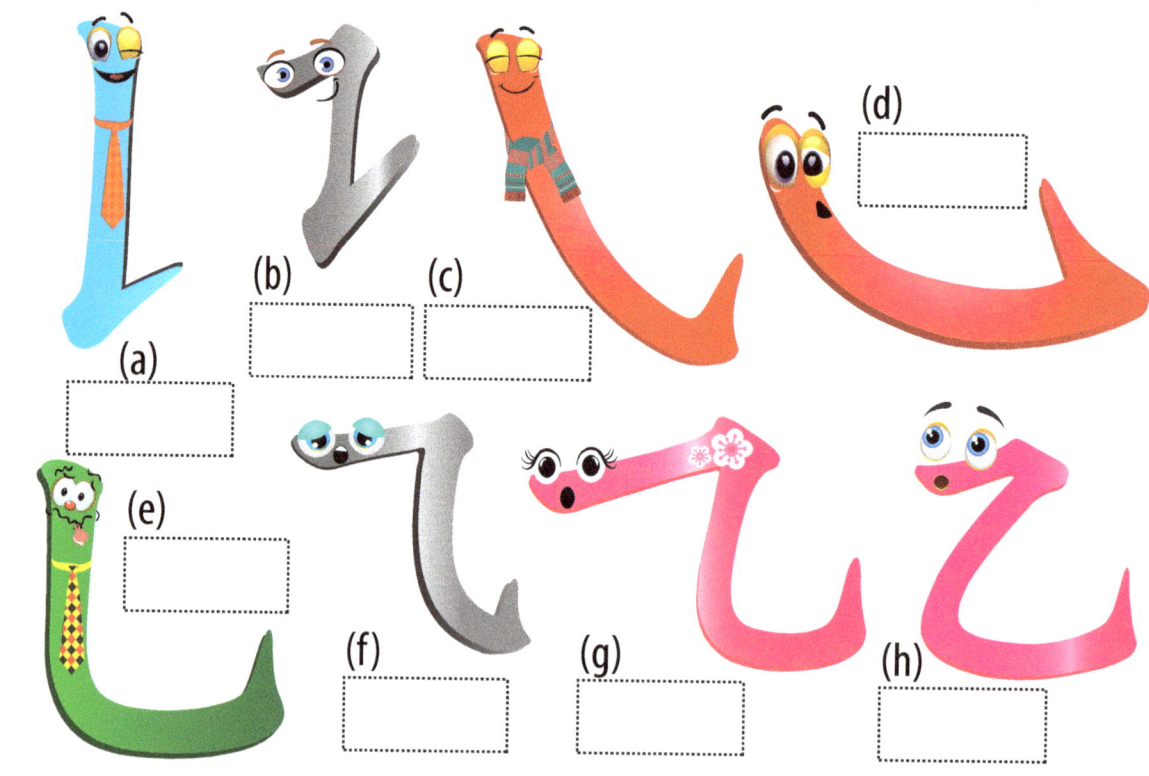

(a) ☐ (b) ☐ (c) ☐ (d) ☐ (e) ☐ (f) ☐ (g) ☐ (h) ☐

After you have checked the answers, revise those names you have made mistakes or forgotten.

Without turning back to earlier pages, write the names of the strokes and draw the strokes in the boxes.

1. Merge L-Bend and 7-Bend

2. Merge L-Bend and 7-Hook

3. Merge 7-Bend and L-Bend

4. Merge 7-Bend and Round-L

5. Merge 7-Bend and 7-Bend

6. Merge Acute-7 and 7-Slash

7. Merge Acute-7 and 7-Hook

8. Merge Acute-7 and Round-L

9. Merge Acute-7 and Hunchback

10. Merge Acute-L and Acute-7

After you have checked the answers, revise those names you have made mistakes or forgotten.

Section 4:
Miscellaneous

Application

Revision

Information

Application

Before you can decode characters like a native, practice decoding them using the Anatomy Map.

Anatomy Map summarises what you have learnt and how you can apply them.

1. How to Apply the Triple ABCs Concept
2. Anatomy Map

How to Apply the 'Triple ABCs Concept'

1. Identify Individual Strokes (35 strokes)

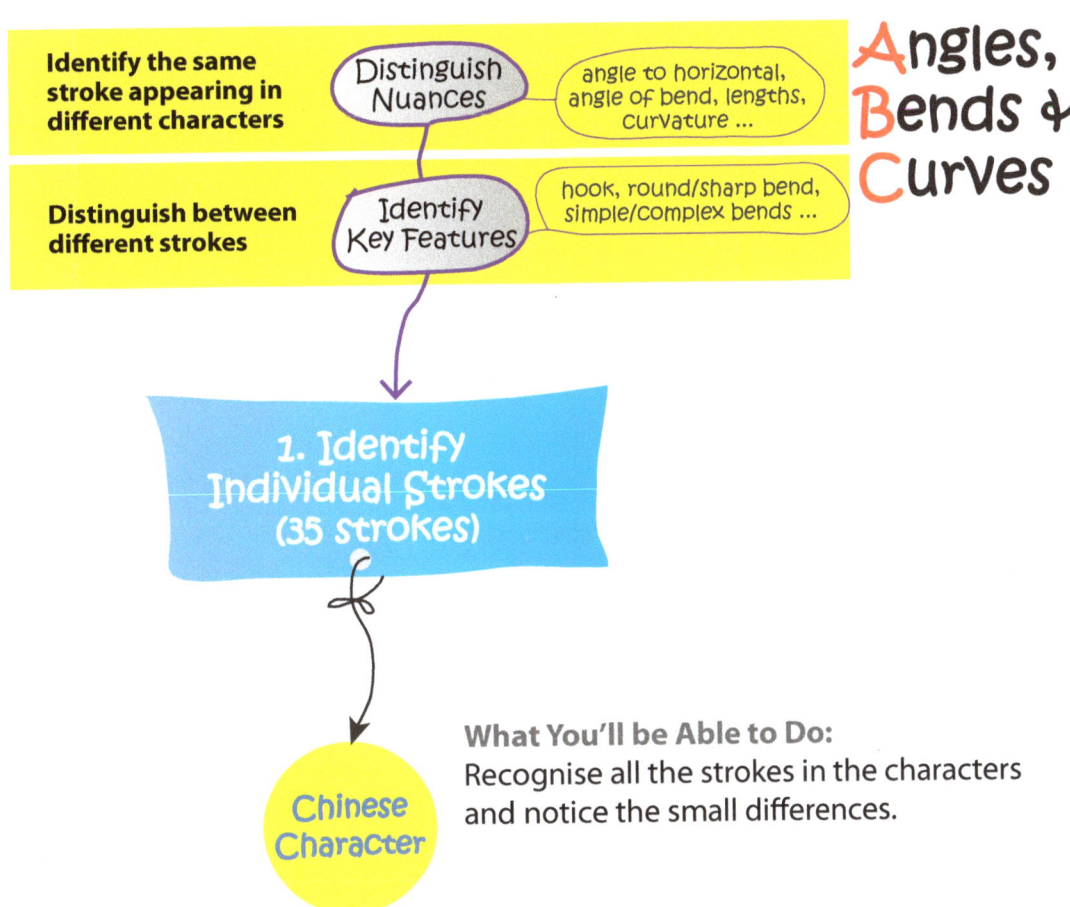

Identify the same stroke appearing in different characters → Distinguish Nuances → angle to horizontal, angle of bend, lengths, curvature ...

Distinguish between different strokes → Identify Key Features → hook, round/sharp bend, simple/complex bends ...

Angles, **B**ends & **C**urves

1. Identify Individual Strokes (35 strokes)

Chinese Character

What You'll be Able to Do:
Recognise all the strokes in the characters and notice the small differences.

How to Apply the 'Triple ABCs Concept'

2. Analyse Stroke Relationships

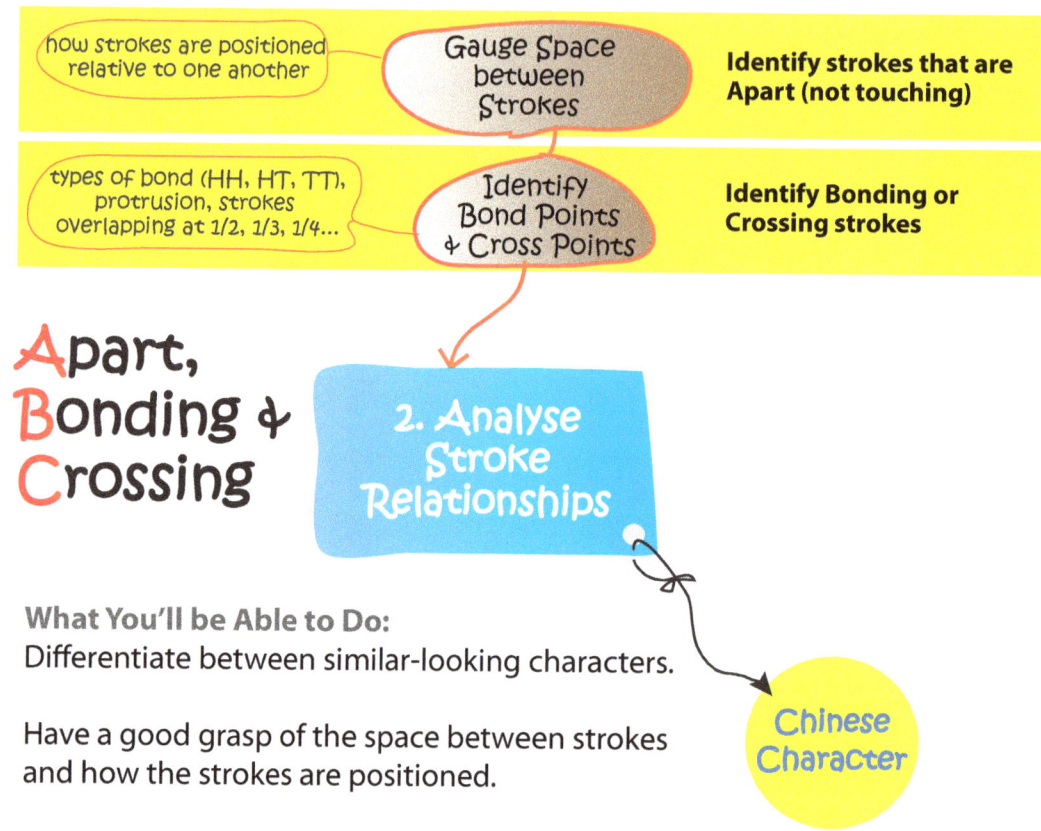

how strokes are positioned relative to one another

Gauge Space between Strokes

Identify strokes that are Apart (not touching)

types of bond (HH, HT, TT), protrusion, strokes overlapping at 1/2, 1/3, 1/4...

Identify Bond Points & Cross Points

Identify Bonding or Crossing strokes

Apart, **B**onding & **C**rossing

2. Analyse Stroke Relationships

Chinese Character

What You'll be Able to Do:
Differentiate between similar-looking characters.

Have a good grasp of the space between strokes and how the strokes are positioned.

NOTE:
More will be covered in the next book on stroke sequence so that you will be able to name the types of bond (HH, HT, TT).

How to Apply the 'Triple ABCs Concept'

3. Identify Adaptations
4. Identify Structure

Adaptation

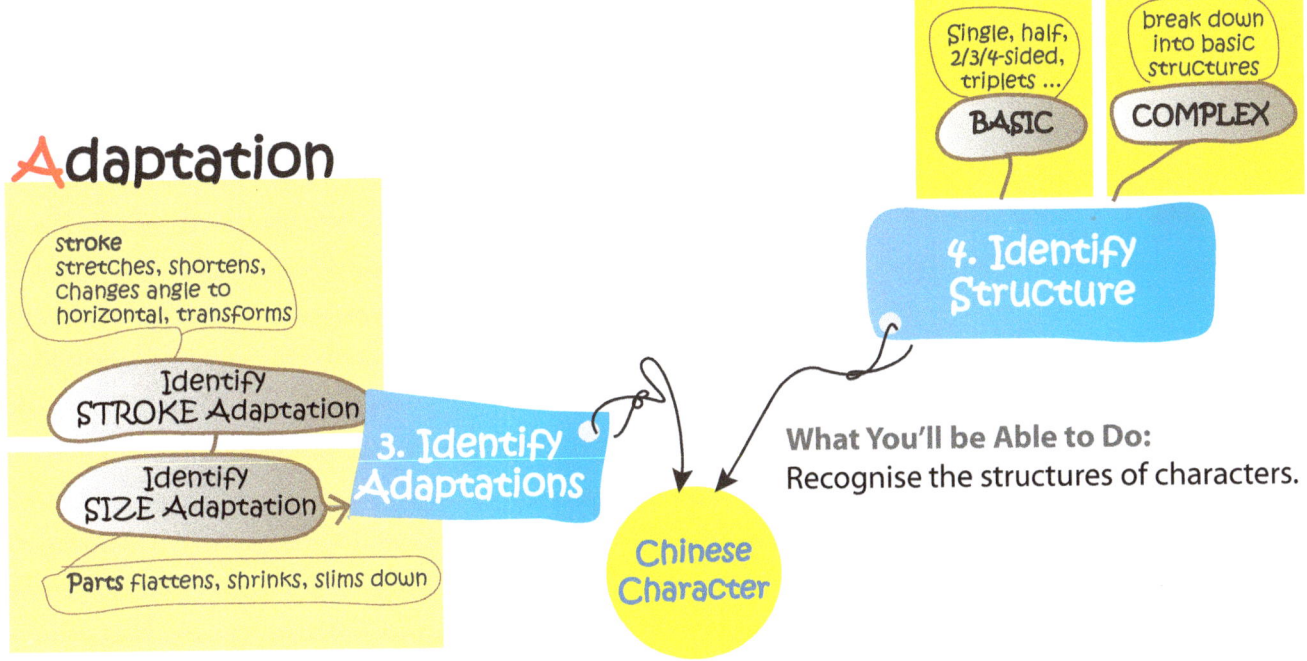

stroke
stretches, shortens,
changes angle to
horizontal, transforms

Identify
STROKE Adaptation

Identify
SIZE Adaptation

Parts flattens, shrinks, slims down

3. Identify Adaptations

Single, half,
2/3/4-sided,
triplets ...

BASIC

break down
into basic
structures

COMPLEX

4. Identify Structure

Chinese Character

What You'll be Able to Do:
Recognise the structures of characters.

What You'll be Able to Do:
Recognise the stroke even if it looks slightly
different in another character and describe
the differences.

How to Apply the 'Triple ABCs Concept'

5. Observe how Strokes/Parts are Balanced

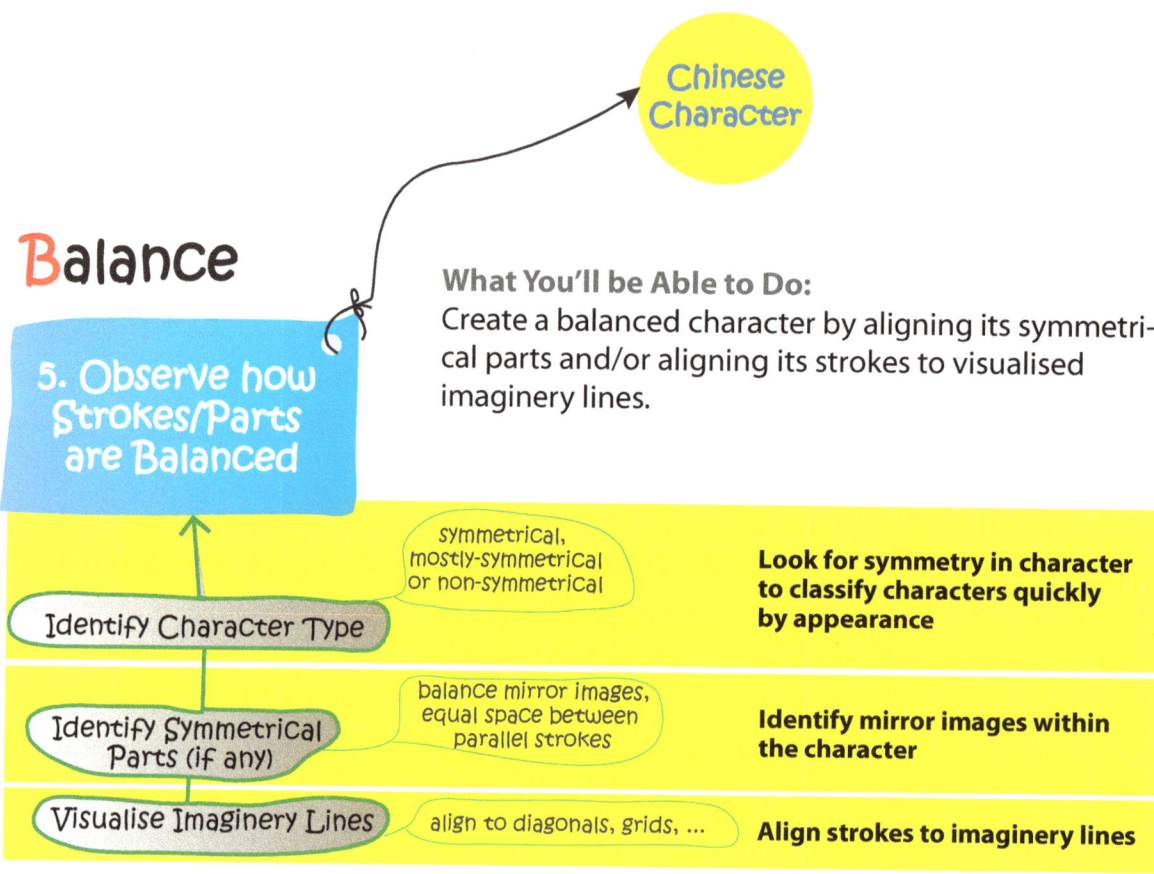

Chinese Character

Balance

5. Observe how Strokes/Parts are Balanced

What You'll be Able to Do:
Create a balanced character by aligning its symmetrical parts and/or aligning its strokes to visualised imaginery lines.

Identify Character Type — symmetrical, mostly-symmetrical or non-symmetrical — **Look for symmetry in character to classify characters quickly by appearance**

Identify Symmetrical Parts (if any) — balance mirror images, equal space between parallel strokes — **Identify mirror images within the character**

Visualise Imaginery Lines — align to diagonals, grids, ... — **Align strokes to imaginery lines**

How to Apply the 'Triple ABCs Concept'

6. Observe how Character is Centred

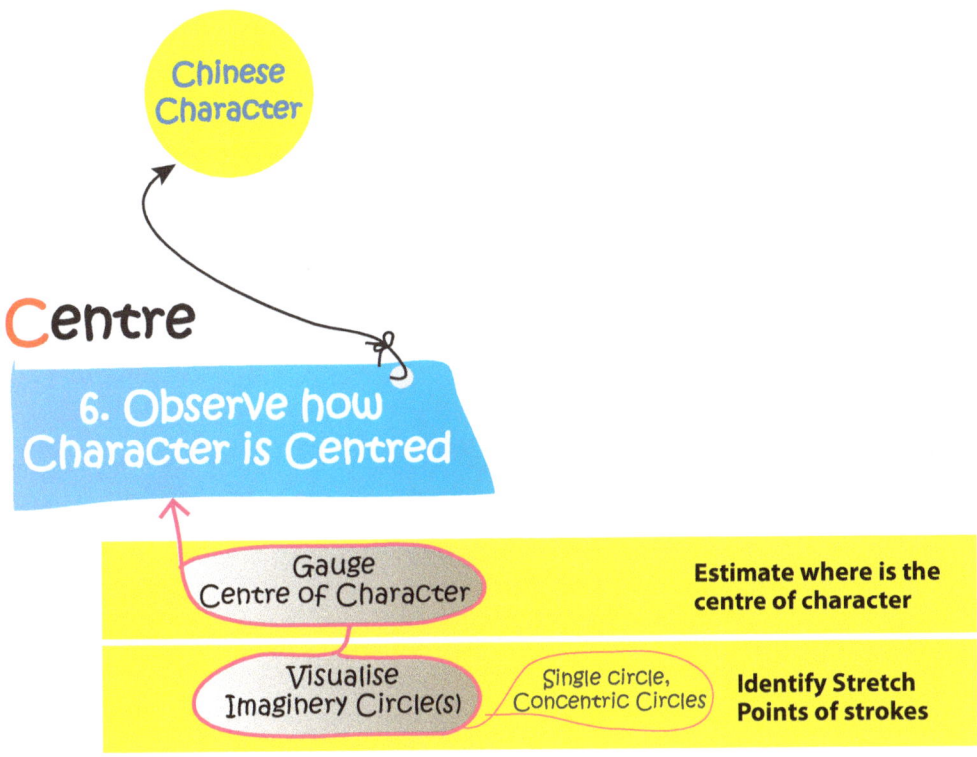

Chinese Character

Centre

6. Observe how Character is Centred

| Gauge Centre of Character | Estimate where is the centre of character |
| Visualise Imaginery Circle(s) — Single circle, Concentric Circles | Identify Stretch Points of strokes |

What You'll be Able to Do:
Create a character that look balanced and centred by positioning strokes with reference to the
- visualised centre of character and
- stretch points on visualised imaginery circle(s).

How to Apply the 'Triple ABCs Concept'

7. Visualise Shape of Character

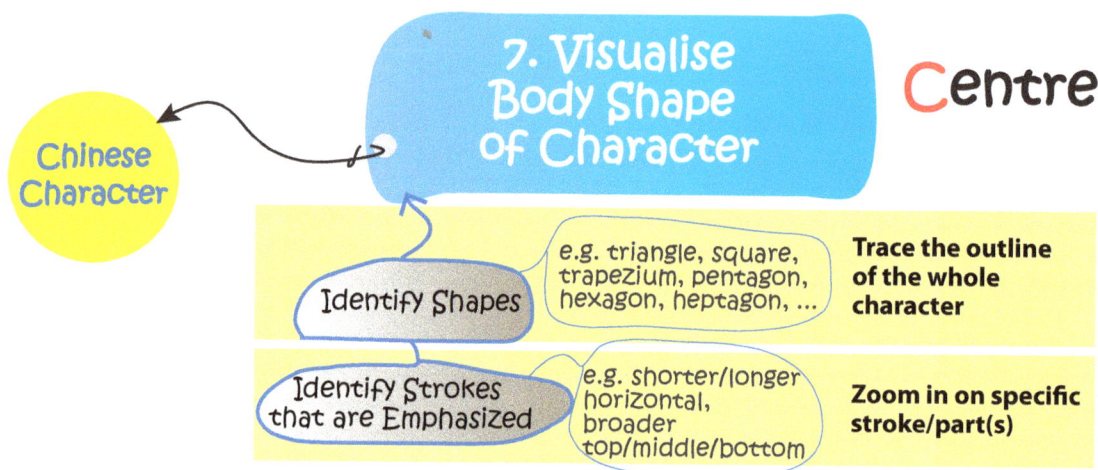

What You'll be Able to Do:
Recognise quickly the relative lengths and positions of strokes and parts by visualising the character's body shape.

How to Apply the 'Triple ABCs Concept'

Angles, Bends & Curves

Distinguish Nuances — angle to horizontal, angle of bend, lengths, curvature ...

Identify Key Features — hook, round/sharp bend, simple/complex bends ...

how strokes are positioned relative to one another

Gauge Space between Strokes

Identify Bond Points & Cross Points — types of bond (HH, HT, TT), protrusion, strokes overlapping at 1/2, 1/3, 1/4...

Apart, Bonding & Crossing

Single, half, 2/3/4-sided, triplets ...

break down into basic structures

BASIC   **COMPLEX**

1. Identify Individual Strokes (35 strokes)

2. Analyse Stroke Relationships

4. Identify Structure

stroke stretches, shortens, changes angle to horizontal, transforms

Adaptation

Identify STROKE Adaptation

Identify SIZE Adaptation

Parts flattens, shrinks, slims down

3. Identify Adaptations

Chinese Character

7. Visualise Body Shape of Character

Identify Shapes — e.g. triangle, square, trapezium, pentagon, hexagon, heptagon, ...

Identify Strokes that are Emphasized — e.g. shorter/longer horizontal, broader top/middle/bottom

Balance

5. Observe how Strokes/Parts are Balanced

Centre

6. Observe how Character is Centred

symmetrical, mostly-symmetrical or non-symmetrical

Identify Character Type

Identify Symmetrical Parts (if any) — balance mirror images, equal space between parallel strokes

Visualise Imaginery Lines — align to diagonals, grids, ...

Gauge Centre of Character

Visualise Imaginery Circle(s) — Single circle, Concentric Circles

'Learn Chinese Characters Without Writing' by W.Q. BLOSH

Learn Chinese *without* WRITING   **175**

Anatomy Map of Chinese Characters

How to Apply

Do I need to apply all the concepts in 'Triple ABCs Concept' to analyse every character?
The Triple ABCs Concept provides you with tools and ways to analyse characters. Pick and choose those that are relevant in that context. Start with tools and methods that you are most comfortable with.

What can the Anatomy Map be used for?
Sample templates provided here. Feel free to modify them based on your needs. You can use the Anatomy Map to do the following:

Anatomy Map Activities
1. Activity 38: Analyse Vocabulary
2. Activity 39: Compare Twinlike Characters
3. Activity 40: Analyse Characters You Choose

Anatomy of Chinese Characters

Complete this Anatomy Map before checking the version we create at the back.

5. Types of Interactions

Apart
Bonding
Crossing

B Bond point
C Cross point

Show the Bond points and Cross points in the diagram.

2. No. of strokes
_____ strokes each

3. Angle to horiztonal
RL-Slash of (1): _____ °
RL-Slash of (3): _____ °

1. Types of Strokes
1) Vertical   (2)
2) _____ ( )
3) _____ ( )
4) _____ ( )
5) _____ ( )
6) _____ ( )
7) _____ ( )

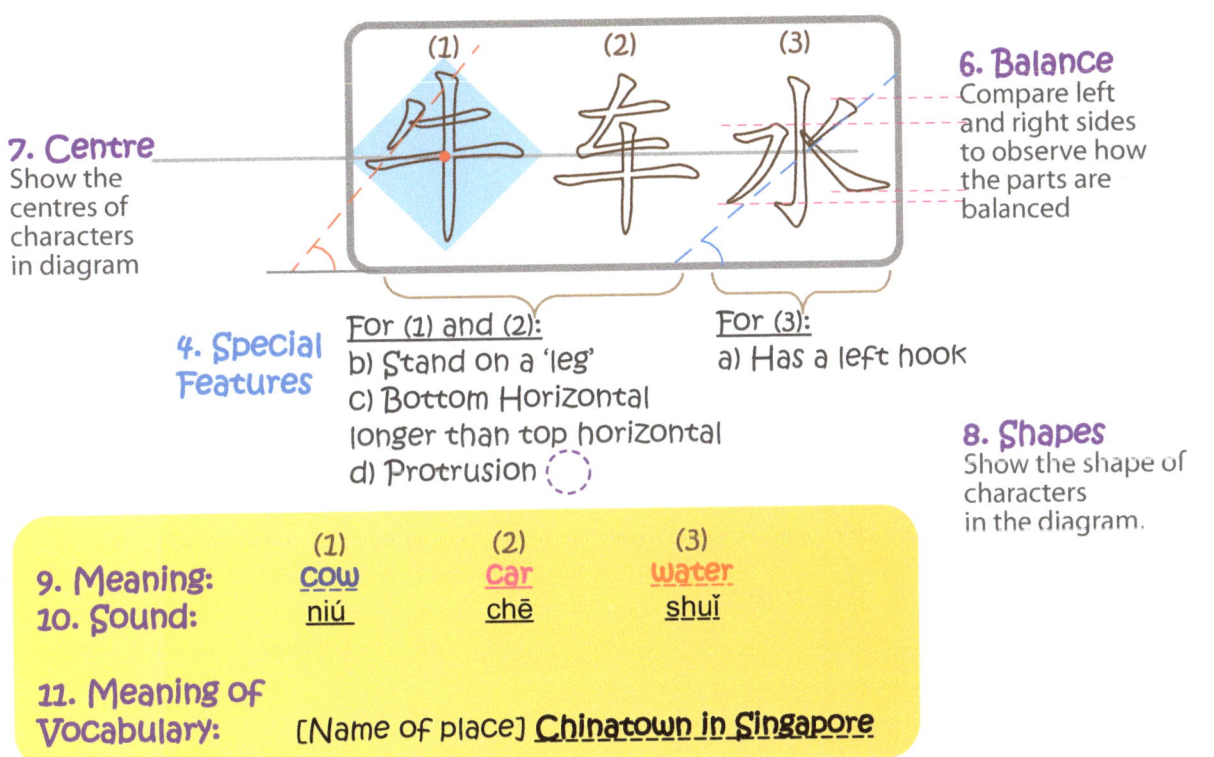

7. Centre
Show the centres of characters in diagram

6. Balance
Compare left and right sides to observe how the parts are balanced

For (1) and (2):
b) Stand on a 'leg'
c) Bottom Horizontal longer than top horizontal
d) Protrusion

For (3):
a) Has a left hook

4. Special Features

8. Shapes
Show the shape of characters in the diagram.

	(1)	(2)	(3)
9. Meaning:	cow	car	water
10. Sound:	niú	chē	shuǐ

11. Meaning of Vocabulary: [Name of place] **Chinatown in Singapore**

Activity 39 Compare Twinlike Characters

Anatomy of Chinese Characters

Complete this Anatomy Map. Distinguish these two similar-looking characters.

5. Types of Interactions

Apart
Bonding
Crossing

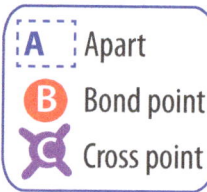

A ┆ Apart

B Bond point

C Cross point

2. No. of strokes
7 Strokes each

3. Angle to horiztonal
_____
_____
_____
_____

1. Types of Strokes
1) Vertical Left Hook (2)
2) Horizontal (3)
3) RL-Slash (3)
4) Leanback (2)
5) RL-Dot (2)
6) Tick (2)

6. Balance

7. Centre

8. Shapes

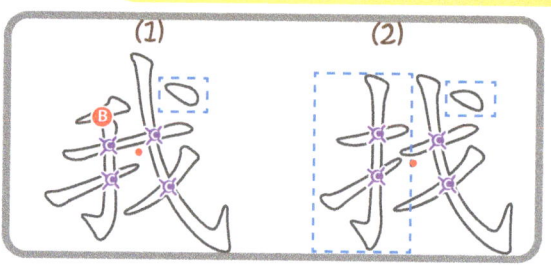

(1)   (2)

4. Special Features

	(1)	(2)
9. Meaning:	I, me	find
10. Sound:	wǒ	zhǎo

© Learn Chinese Characters Without Writing by W.Q. BLOSH

Activity 40 Analyse Any Characters

Anatomy of Chinese Characters
Applying Triple ABCs Concept

Use this template to analyse Chinese characters.

5. Types of Interactions
Apart
Bonding
Crossing

B — Bond point
C — Cross point

2. No. of strokes
_____

3. Angle to horiztonal
_____
_____
_____
_____

1. Types of Strokes
1) _____
2) _____
3) _____
4) _____
5) _____
6) _____
7) _____
8) _____
9) _____
10) _____

6. Balance

7. Centre

8. Shapes

4. Special Features

9. Meaning:
_____

10. Sound:
_____

11. Meaning of Vocabulary:
_____

© Learn Chinese Characters Without Writing by W.Q. BLOSH

Revision

Revision activities on the 35 strokes were provided at the end of each section.

In this section, more revision activites are provided to help you remember the strokes in different ways.

Complete all the activities or select any activity based on your interest.

1. Strokes Bubble Map

2. My Cartoon Canvas

3. My Visual Organiser

The stroke in the 'white bubble' is created by combining the strokes in the 'blue bubble(s)' attached to it. Fill in the missing strokes.

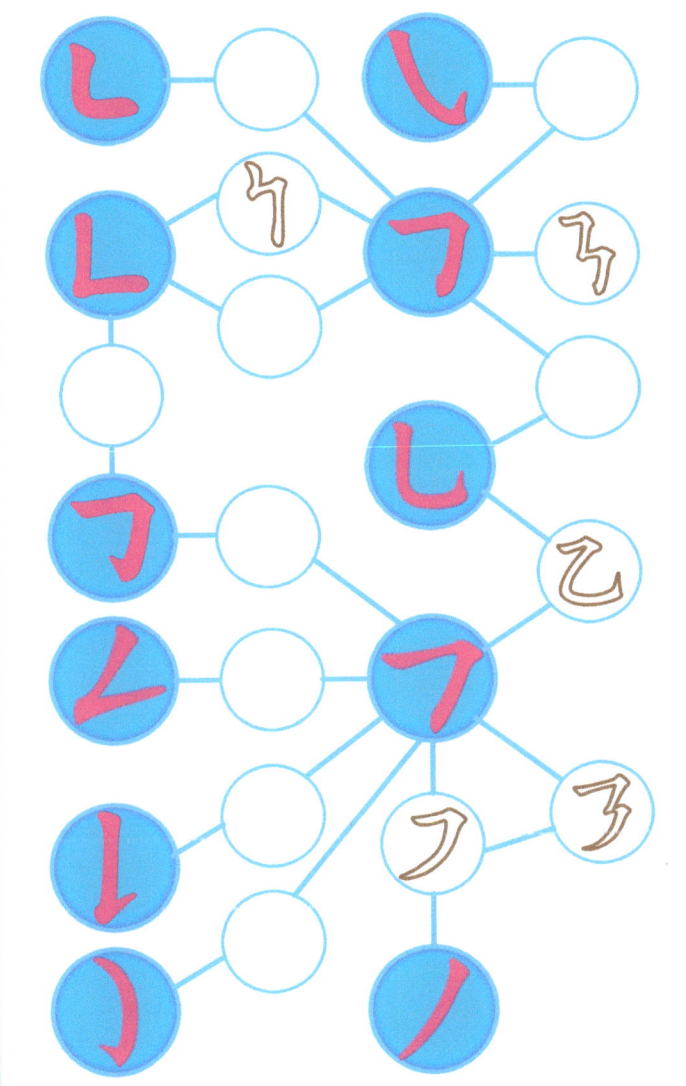

Strokes Bubble Map

Fill in the remaining 10 strokes that did not appear in the bubble map. Altogether, there are 35 strokes.

STRAIGHT FAMILY

○ ○ ○ ○

CURVE FAMILY

○ ○

DOT FAMILY

○ ○ ○

BEND FAMILY

○

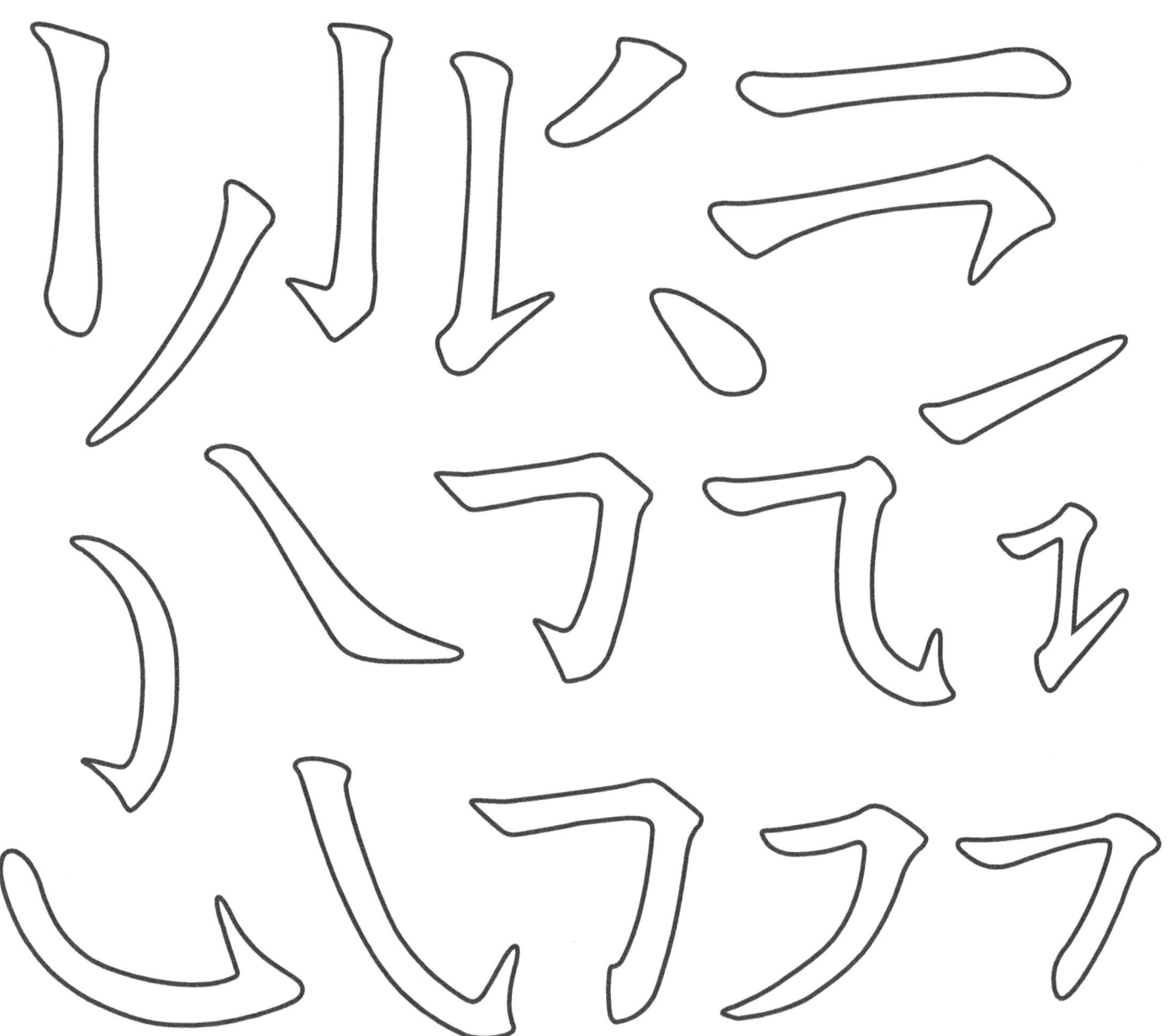

Create your own cartoons of the strokes. What does each stroke remind you of? Transform them into cartoon characters, colour them, write their names, make notes besides each of them ...

My Cartoon Canvas

Activity 43

Draw the remaining strokes into the different sectors of the circle according to the families they belong.

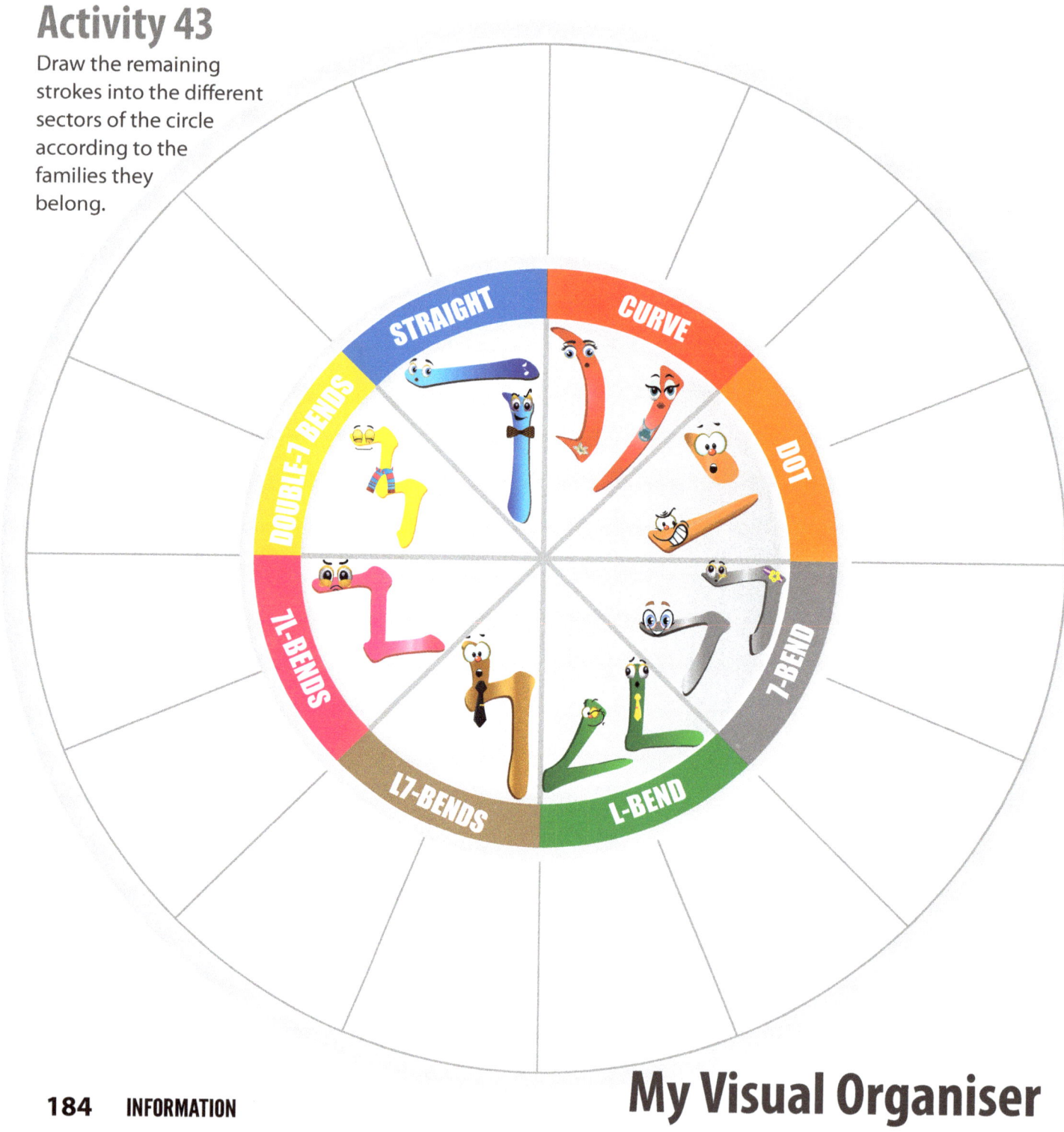

My Visual Organiser

Information

This section provides additional information to help you do the activities.

Basic Geometry

How to Use a Protractor

Read angle measurement here

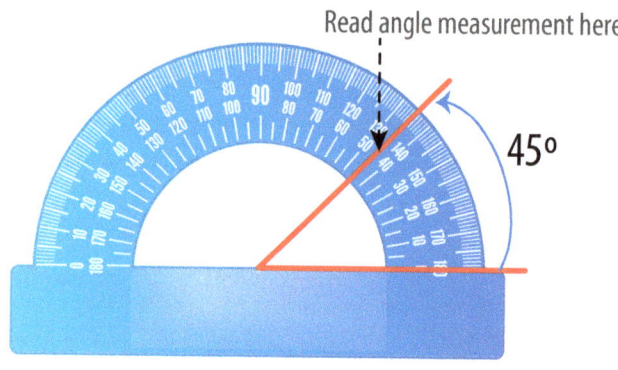

45°

Two Types of Set Square

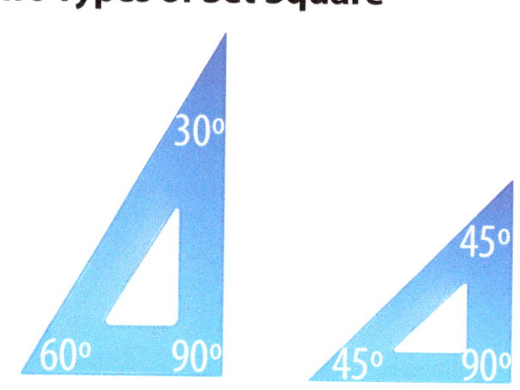

30°

60° 90°

45°

45° 90°

Draw Circle with a Compass

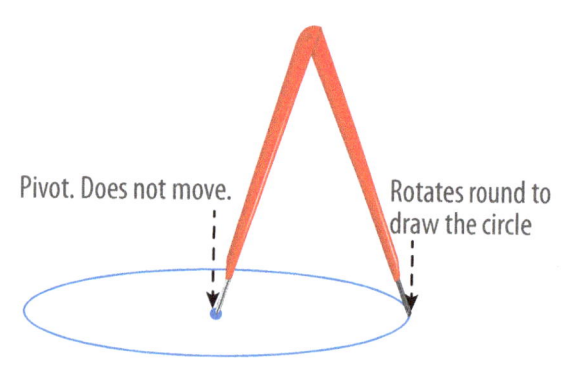

Pivot. Does not move.

Rotates round to draw the circle

Draw Parallel Lines with Set Squares

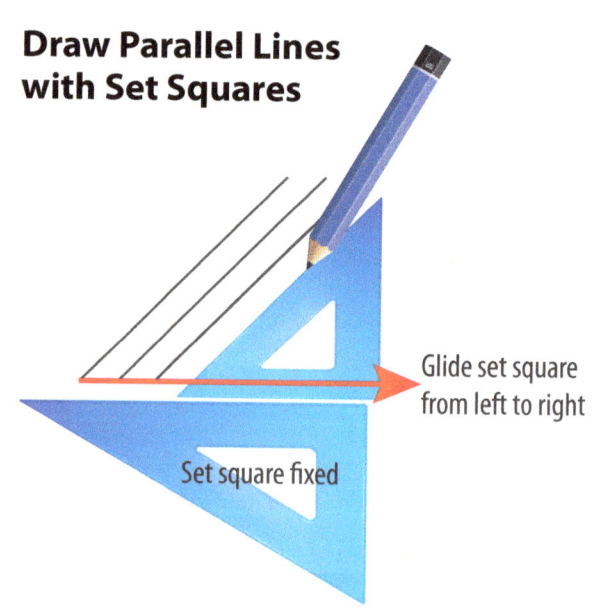

Glide set square from left to right

Set square fixed

Construct Angles with a Compass

1) Construct 90° angle

Continues...

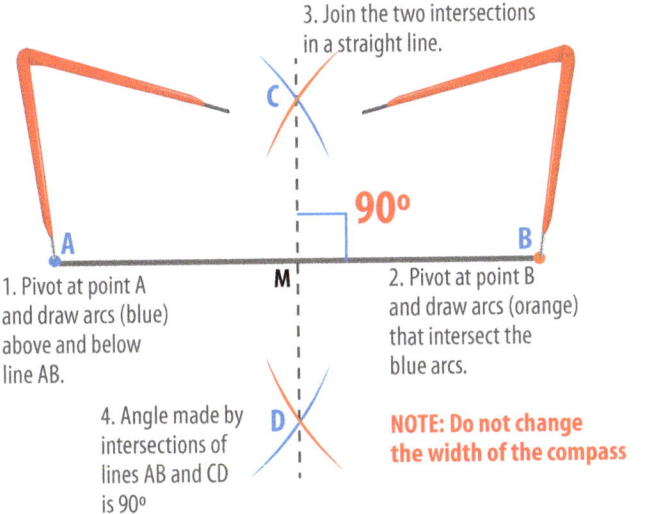

3. Join the two intersections in a straight line.

90°

1. Pivot at point A and draw arcs (blue) above and below line AB.

2. Pivot at point B and draw arcs (orange) that intersect the blue arcs.

4. Angle made by intersections of lines AB and CD is 90°

NOTE: Do not change the width of the compass

2) Construct 45° angle

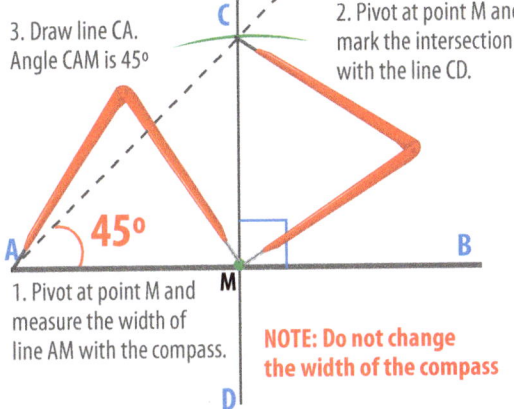

3. Draw line CA. Angle CAM is 45°

2. Pivot at point M and mark the intersection with the line CD.

45°

1. Pivot at point M and measure the width of line AM with the compass.

NOTE: Do not change the width of the compass

3) Construct 60° angle

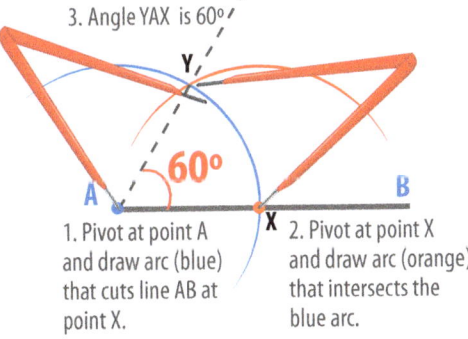

3. Angle YAX is 60°

60°

1. Pivot at point A and draw arc (blue) that cuts line AB at point X.

2. Pivot at point X and draw arc (orange) that intersects the blue arc.

NOTE: Do not change the width of the compass

Continues...

4) Construct 30° angle

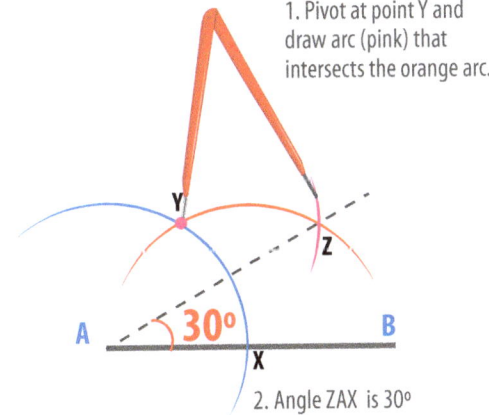

1. Pivot at point Y and draw arc (pink) that intersects the orange arc.

30°

2. Angle ZAX is 30°

Applying Geometry to Chinese

For some of the activities in this book, you can solve them in more than one way. For example, to solve Activities 2 to 4, you can try the methods listed here.

 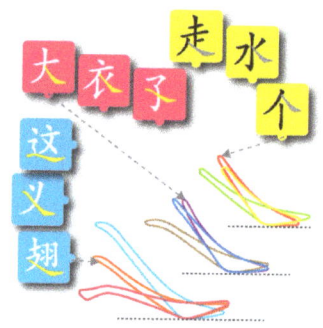 

A) Measure the strokes' angles to the horizontal:

1. Do precise measurements of the angles using a **PROTRACTOR**

2. Use the usual two types of **SET SQUARE** as shown to gauge the angles.

3. Use a **COMPASS** to construct different angles

4. Use your naked eyes to do the comparison (if you used only this method, try the other methods listed here).

5. Use a **magnifying glass** if you need to enlarge them to see better for comparison

6. For those who are savvy with technology, take digital photographs of the characters and strokes and do comparison in your electronic devices.

7. For those with 'itchy fingers' (meaning you like to destroy things), cut out the strokes and characters and compare them.

B) Measure the lengths of the strokes:

8. Use a ruler to estimate their lengths.

9. Use a thread to measure along the curvature (more accurate then using a ruler).

C) Gauge / draw the curvature of the stroke

10. Use a compass

11. Use a geometric template ruler for circles

12. Use bottle caps of different sizes (or anything that is round) to draw circles on the paper.

13. Use a curve ruler

We have listed so many ways to do the activity. If you have not tried any of them, redo the activities using these methods. Use your creativity to think of more ways to solve them.

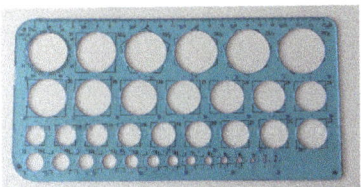

Geometric Template Ruler

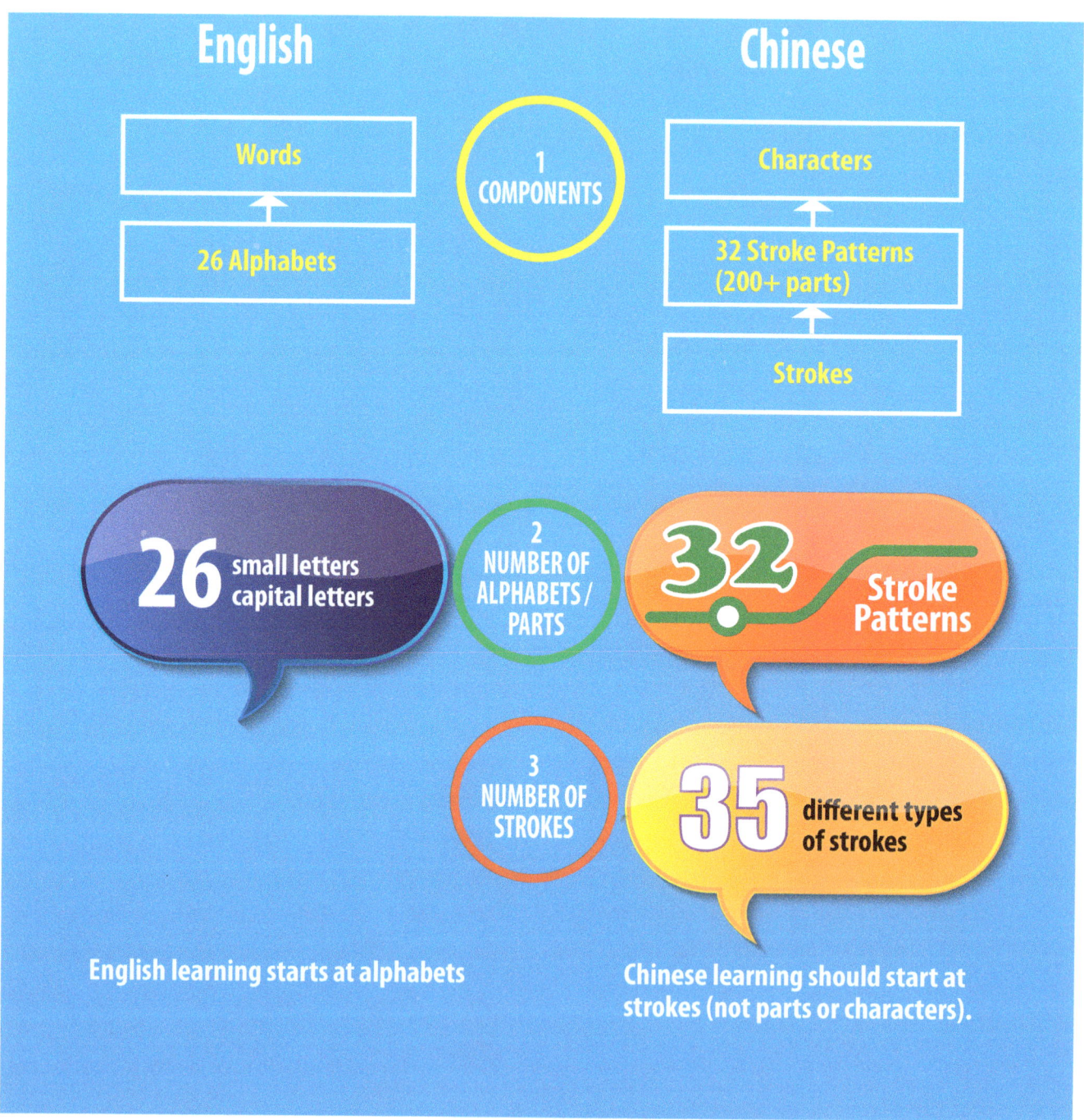

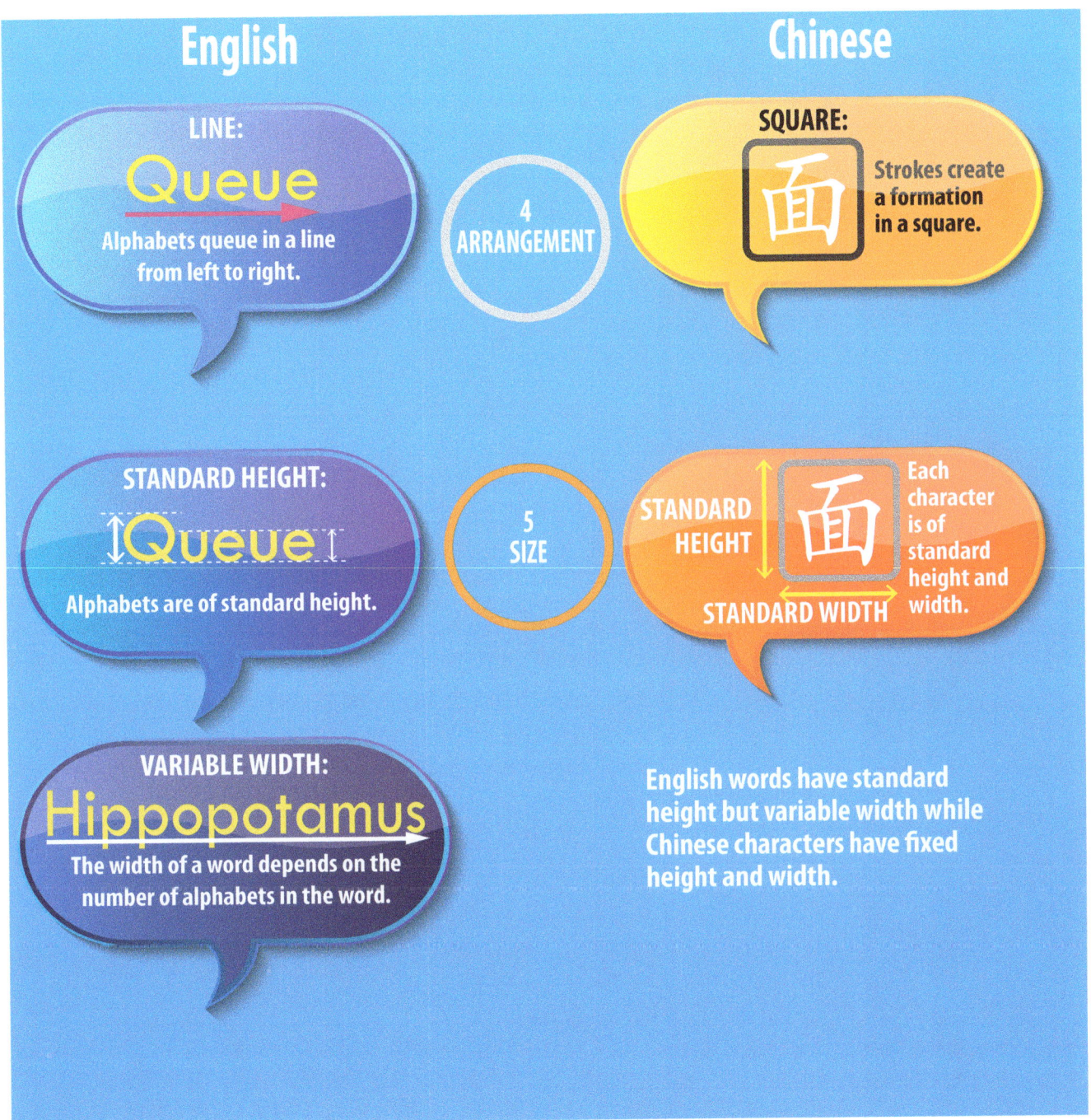

English

EQUAL SPACE
between Alphabets:

Queue

EXPANDABLE SPACE:

pneumonoul...

The length of English word can get as long as it wants.

Chinese

VARIABLE SPACE
between Strokes:

Space between strokes varies in different characters

NON-EXPANDABLE SPACE:

乙　挤

Every character has a fixed space regardless of the number of strokes

6 SPACE

The space an English word occupies is infinite, depending on the number of alphabets in the word.

The space a Chinese character occupies is finite regardless of the number of strokes.

Within an English word, the spaces between alphabets are the same.

Within a Chinese character, the spaces between the strokes are variable.

松 ✗ *Too spaced out*　挤 ✗ *Too squeezy*

松 ✓ *Just right!*　挤 ✓ *Just right!*

192

English | Chinese

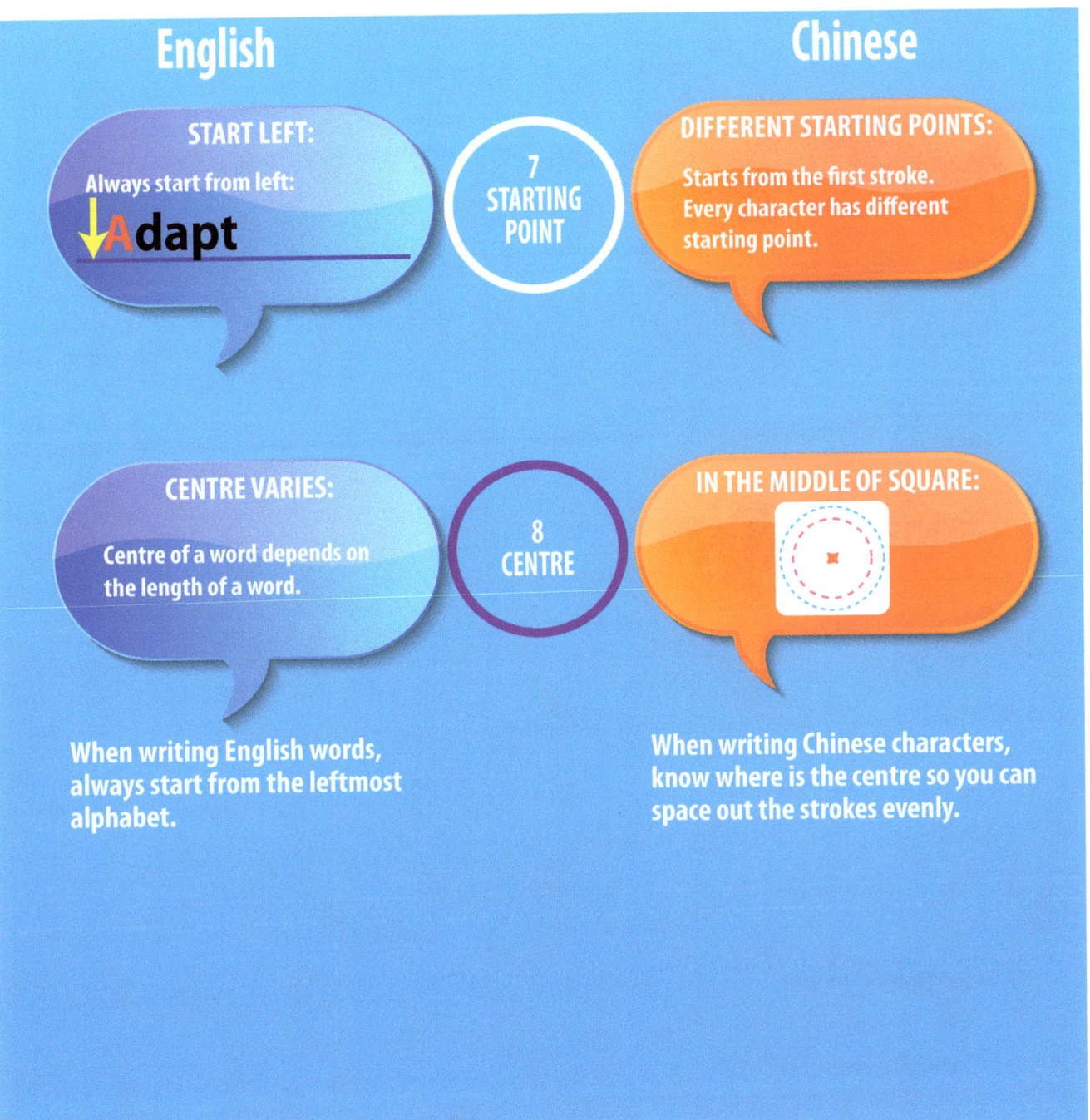

START LEFT:

Always start from left:

↓Adapt

7 STARTING POINT

DIFFERENT STARTING POINTS:

Starts from the first stroke. Every character has different starting point.

CENTRE VARIES:

Centre of a word depends on the length of a word.

8 CENTRE

IN THE MIDDLE OF SQUARE:

When writing English words, always start from the leftmost alphabet.

When writing Chinese characters, know where is the centre so you can space out the strokes evenly.

Chinese Names of Strokes

1. Vertical — **shù**	14. 7-Bend — **héng zhé**	25. L7-Bends — **shù zhé zhé**
2. Vertical Left — **shù gōu**	15. 7-Hook — **héng zhé gōu**	26. L7-Hook — **shù zhé zhé gōu**
3. Vertical Right — **shù tí**	16. 7-Leanback — **héng xié gōu**	27. Lightning — **shù zhé piě**
4. Horizontal — **héng**	17. Acute-7	28. 7L-Bends — **héng zhé zhé**
5. Horizontal Hook — **héng gōu**	18. 7-Slash — **héng piě**	29. Round-7L — **héng zhé wān**
6. RL-Dot / 7. LR-Dot — **diǎn**	19. 7-Back kick — **héng zhé tí**	30. 7L-Hook — **héng zhé wān gōu**
8. Tick — **tí**	20. L-Bend — **shù zhé**	31. Z-Hook
9. RL-Slash — **piě**	21. Round-L — **shù wān**	32. Double-7 Bends — **héng zhé zhé zhé**
10. LR-Slash — **nà**	22. L-Hook — **shù wān gōu**	33. Double-7 Hook — **héng zhé zhé zhé gōu**
11. Hunchback — **wān gōu**	23. Boomerang — **piě diǎn**	34. Double-7 Slash — **héng zhé zhé piě**
12. Leanback — **xié gōu**	24. Acute-L — **piě zhé**	35. Acute-7 Hunchback — **héng piě wān gōu**
13. Curl-up — **wò gōu**		

194

Answers

Activity 1

Activity 2

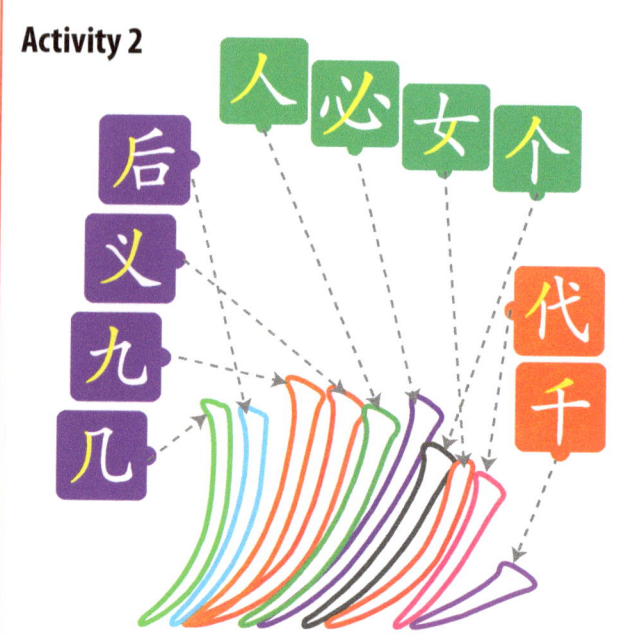

Activity 3

Activity 4

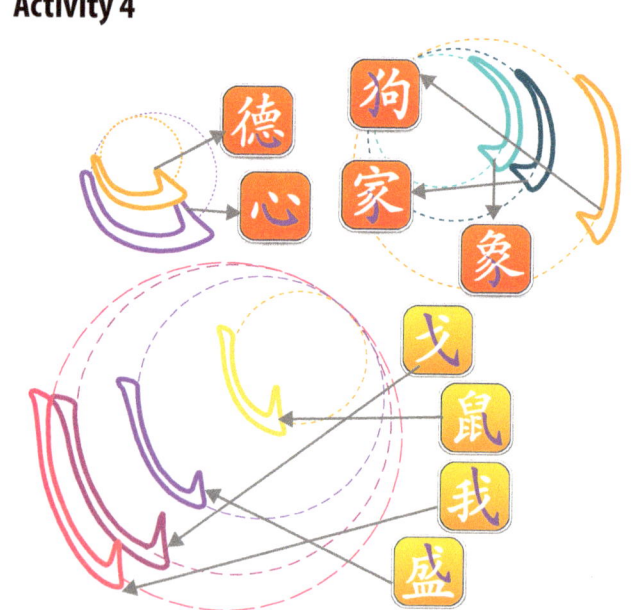

Activity 5

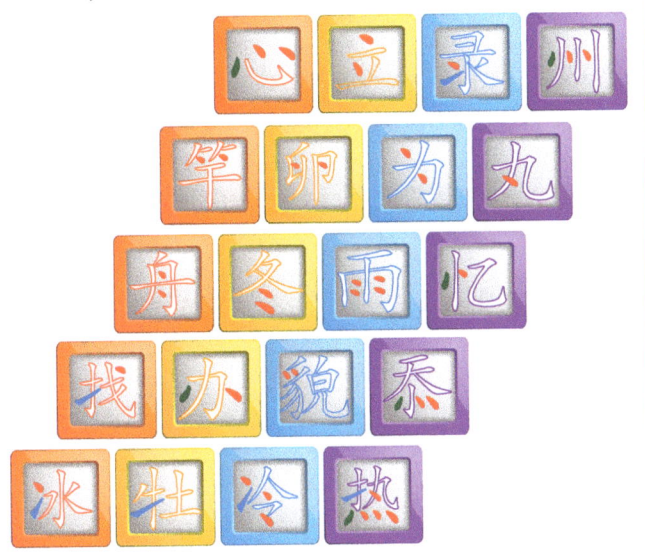

Activity 6

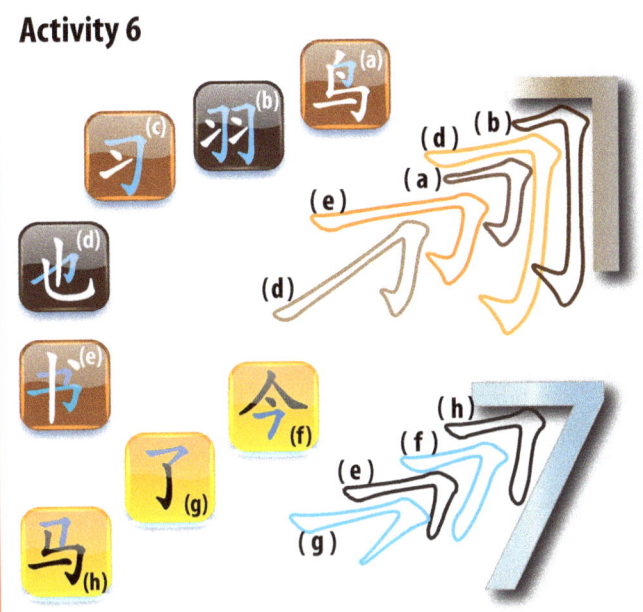

Activity 7

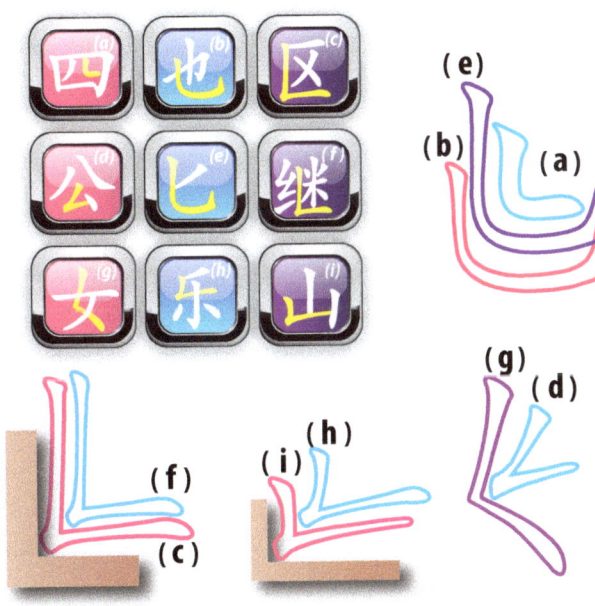

Activity 8

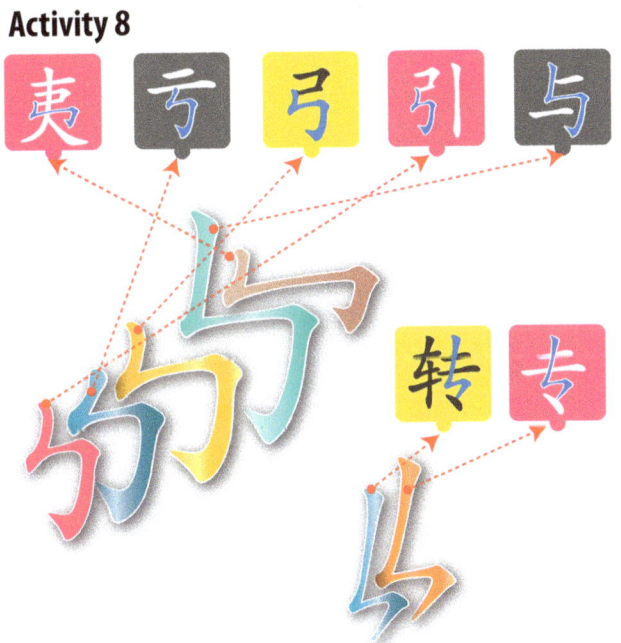

Activity 9

九 (a)
九 (b)
虬 (c)

(d)
(c)
(e)
(f)

气 (d)
飞 (e)
讯 (f)

(g)
(h)
(a)
(b)

瓦 (g)
几 (h)

Activity 10

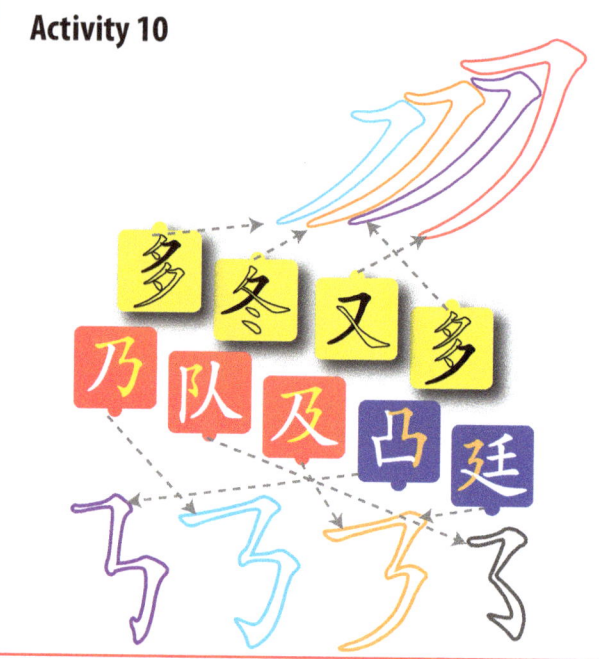

多 冬 又 多
乃 队 及 凸 廷

Activity 11

Highlight *7-Bend* in these characters:

枣 互 丑 唐 兼
典
與
b) Highlight *L7-Hook*
骂
号 写 弟 号 弯 考

Highlight *7 Hook* in these characters:

d) Highlight *Double-7 Hook:*

却 那 厉 丽 局 册
奶
汤
隽 秀

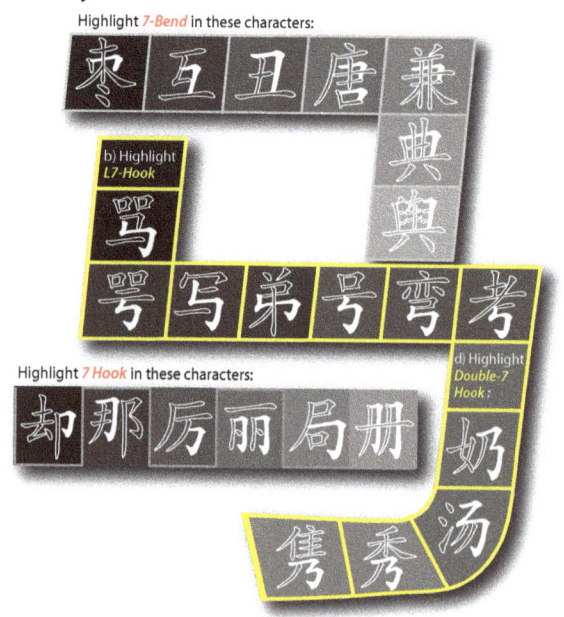

Activity 12

Highlight *Acute 7* in these characters:

了 乏 今 甬 角 予 学

Highlight *L-Bend :*
收
击
匹
出

Highlight *Acute-L :*
台 允 玄
框 每 发 流
亥
参

Highlight *7-Slash* in these characters:

友 受 最 麦 处 复 夜

Activity 13

Highlight *7-Leanback*:

飞 虱 汽 风 氘 迅

Highlight *L-Hook*:

犯 记 旨 见 先 光 兔

Highlight *7L-Hook*:

冗 亮 凡 秃 瓷 究

Highlight *Z-hook*:

艺 疙

Highlight *7-Back kick*:

话 赢

瓦

Activity 14

五 风 爱 甫 话

7-Bend
7-Hook
7-Leanback
Acute-7
7-Slash
7-Back kick

池 客 兜 氛 令

Activity 15

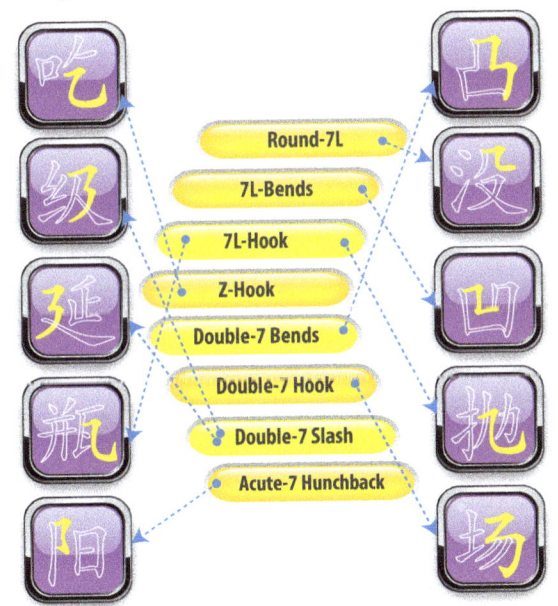

吃 级 延 瓶 阳

Round-7L
7L-Bends
7L-Hook
Z-Hook
Double-7 Bends
Double-7 Hook
Double-7 Slash
Acute-7 Hunchback

凸 没 凷 抛 场

Activity 16

毛 世 危 如 传 舞

L-Hook
L-Bend
Round-L
Boomerang
Acute-L
L7-Bends
L7-Hook
Acute-L7

巡 军 弗 鼎 焉 丙

Activity 17

Activity 18

Activity 19

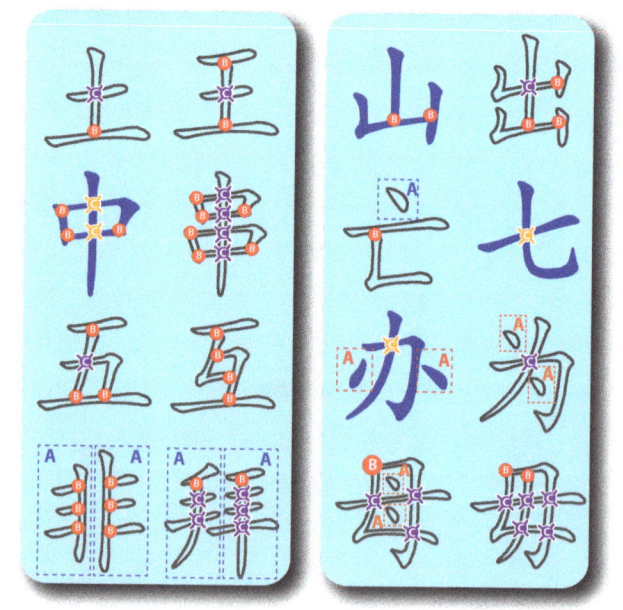

Activity 20

Activity 21

1. L7-Bends
2. Horizontal and Z-Hook
3. Boomerang
4. Hunchback
5. Tick
6. 7L-Bends
7. L-Bend
8. Acute-L7/Lightning
9. Acute-7 Hunchback
10. Leanback and 7-Bend
11. Double-7 Slash
12. Double-7 Hook
13. Curl-up
14. L-Hook
15. 7-Leanback

Activity 22

语 晶 天 平
吉 号 刀 句
朋 街 趁 庆
函 风 匠 国

(m) 函 (f) 号 (b) 晶 (p) 国 (j) 街 (g) 刀
(e) 吉 (k) 趁 (d) 平 (o) 匠 (a) 语 (i) 朋
(c) 天 (l) 庆 (n) 风 (h) 句

Activity 23

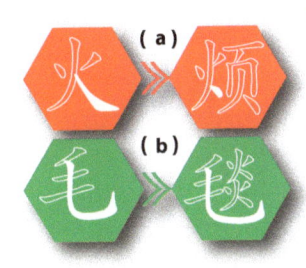

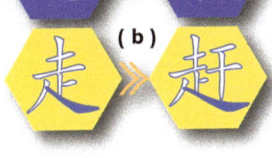

a) Shorten Stroke
b) Stretch Horizontally
c) Horizontal to Tick
d) L-Hook to Vertical Right Hook

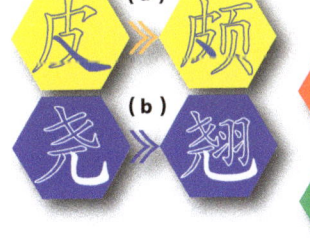

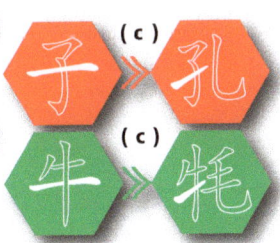

Activity 24

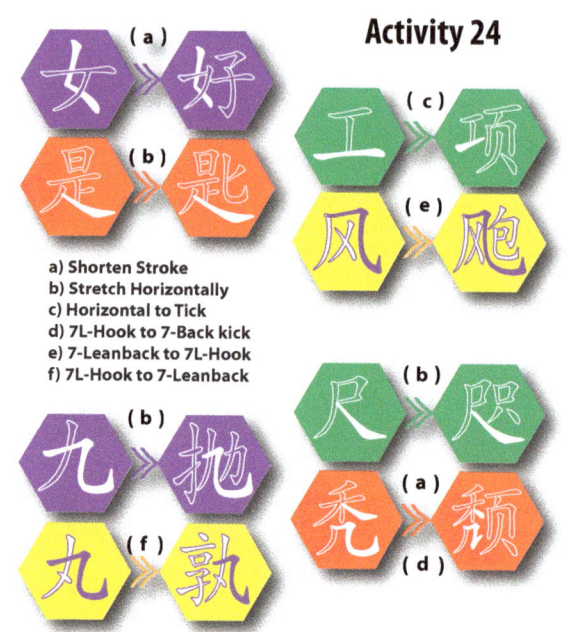

a) Shorten Stroke
b) Stretch Horizontally
c) Horizontal to Tick
d) 7L-Hook to 7-Back kick
e) 7-Leanback to 7L-Hook
f) 7L-Hook to 7-Leanback

Activity 25

1. LR-Slash becomes **LR-Dot**

2a. 7L-Hook becomes **7-Leanback**

2b. 7L-Hook becomes **7-Back kick**

3. 7-Leanback becomes **7L-Hook**

4. Horizontal becomes **Tick**

5. L-Hook becomes **Vertical Right**

Activity 26

Activity 27

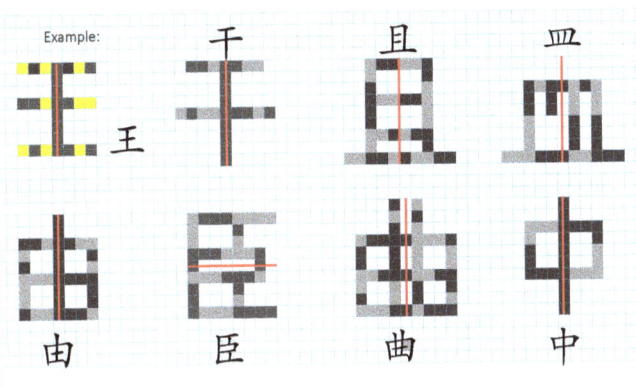

Draw 1 to 2 circles

Draw 3 circles

Draw 4 circles

Activity 31

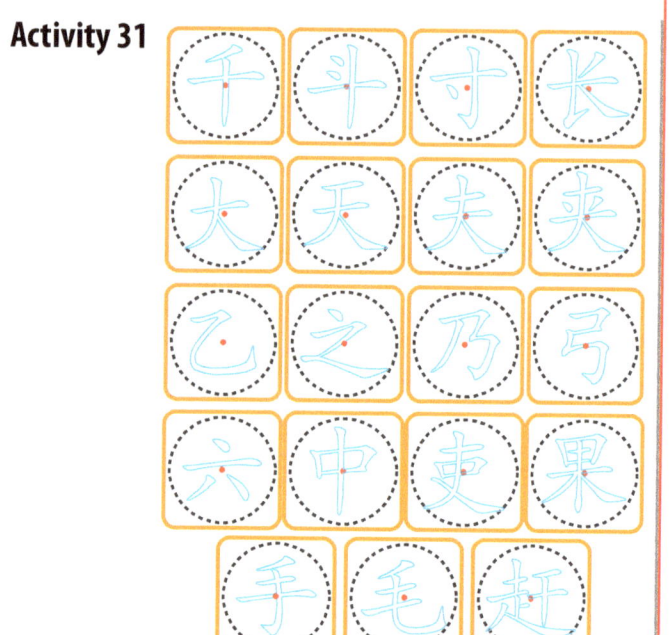

Activity 32

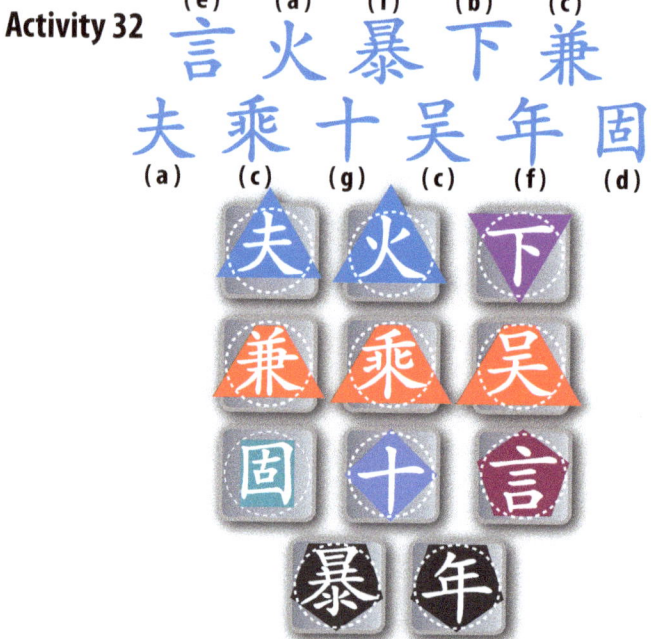

Activity 33

1. 万 方
2. 刀 刃
3. 刁 习
4. 予 矛

5. 勿 匆
6. 同 同
7. 印 印
8. 氏 氐

9. 巾 币
10. 九 丸
11. 几 凡
12. 艮 良

13. 戈 戈
14. 戎 戒
15. 冉 再
16. 乌 鸟

17. 厂 广
18. 卜 下
19. 十 千
20. 干 午

21. 斤 斥
22. 士 壬
23. 夫 失
24. 未 朱

25. 夕 歹
26. 古 舌
27. 又 叉
28. 史 吏

29. 今 令
30. 兰 羊
31. 从 丛
32. 不 丕

33. 火 灭　37. 勺 勾　41. 立 产　45. 李 季

34. 皿 血　38. 日 旧　42. 其 甚　46. 幻 幼

35. 目 自　39. 三 丰　43. 帅 师　47. 亨 享

36. 旦 亘　40. 米 来　44. 代 伐　48. 茶 荼

49. 汁 汗　53. 侯 候　57. 天 关　61. 开 并

50. 坏 环　54. 狼 狼　58. 父 交　62. 卯 卵

51. 故 敌　55. 休 体　59. 买 卖　63. 卓 桌

52. 快 快　56. 人 火　60. 允 充　64. 用 角

65. 巴 色
66. 丹 舟
67. 逐 遂
68. 元 先

69. 垠 琅
70. 受 爱
71. 束 東
72. 六 兴

73. 乖 乘
74. 下 卡
75. 栗 粟
76. 买 实

77. 尺 尽
78. 巨 臣
79. 中 虫
80. 幺 玄

81. 全 金
82. 工 左
83. 山 击
84. 水 丞

85. 且 县
86. 直 真
87. 具 真
88. 盅 盐

89. 壁 璧
90. 吕 昌

Activity 34

91. 岚 岗

92. 着 脊

93. 亭 亮

94. 爪 瓜

95. 前 俞

96. 衣 农

97. 开 井

98. 呈 皇

99. 未 末

100. 东 乐

101. 杖 枚

102. 友 反

103. 伞 平

104. 平 手

105. 刀 力

106. 风 凤

107. 名 各

108. 庄 压

109. 佘 余

110. 义 叉

111. 午 牛

112. 矢 失

113. 水 永

Activity 35

114. 大 天 夭

115. 七 毛 毛

116. 云 去 丢

117. 王 玉 主

118. 业 亚 严

119. 大 太 犬

120. 儿 兀 元

121. 戊 戍 戍

122. 杳 查 香

123. 哀 衰 衷

124. 力 办 为

125. 兄 兑 克

126. 贝 贞 负

127. 口 石 右

128. 己 已 巳

129. 上 止 正

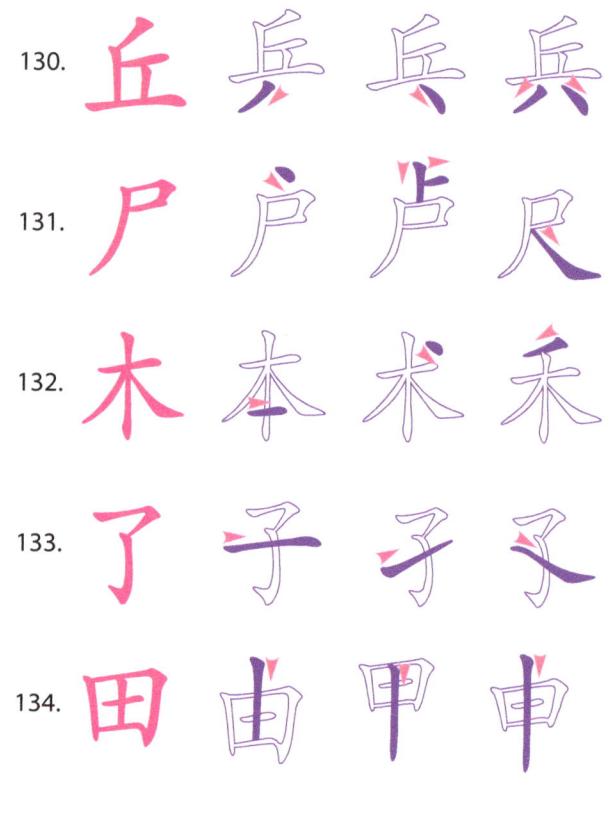

130. 丘 兵 兵 兵
131. 尸 户 卢 尺
132. 木 本 术 禾
133. 了 子 子 孓
134. 田 由 甲 申

Activity 36

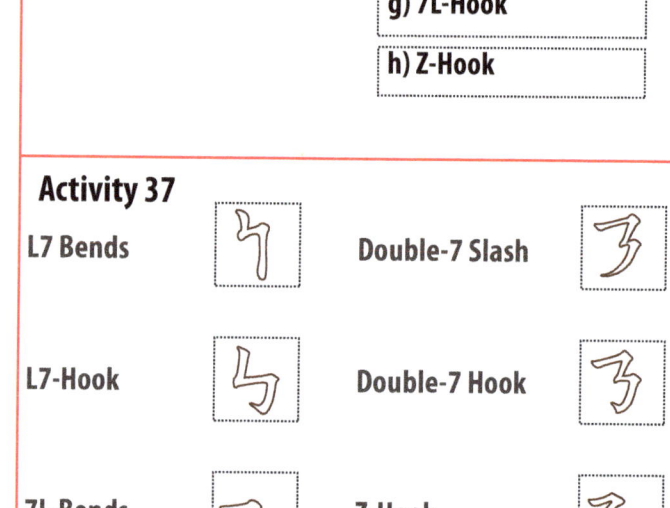

Strokes with Left Hook

a) Vertical Left Hook

b) Hunchback

c) 7-Hook

d) L7-Hook

e) Double-7 Hook

f) Acute-7 Hunchback

Strokes with Right Hook

a) Vertical Right Hook

b) 7-Back kick

c) Leanback

d) Curl-Up

e) L-Hook

f) 7-Leanback

g) 7L-Hook

h) Z-Hook

Activity 37

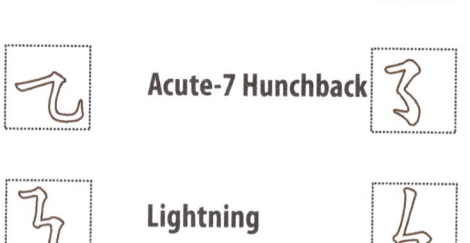

L7 Bends

L7-Hook

7L-Bends

7L-Hook

Double-7 Bends

Double-7 Slash

Double-7 Hook

Z-Hook

Acute-7 Hunchback

Lightning

Our Version of Anatomy Map

5. Types of Interactions

Apart
Bonding
Crossing

B Bond point

C Cross point

2. No. of strokes
4 strokes each

3. Angle to horizontal
RL-Slash of (1): 50°
RL-Slash of (3): 40°

1. Types of Strokes
1) Vertical (2)
2) Vertical Left (1)
3) Horizontal (4)
4) RL-Slash (2)
5) LR-Slash (1)
6) Acute-L (1)
7) 7-Slash (1)

7. Centre
Centres of
characters
& Imaginery
Circles
identified

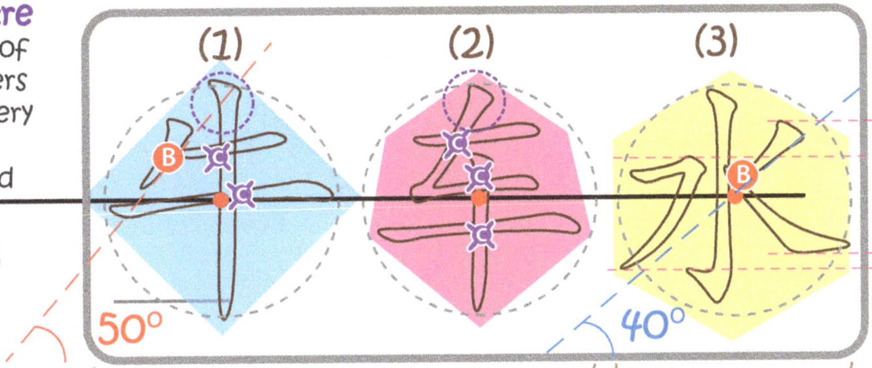

(1)   (2)   (3)

50°   40°

6. Balance
Compare left
and right sides
to observe how
the parts are
balanced

4. Special Features

For (1) and (2):
b) Stand on a 'leg'
c) Bottom Horizontal
longer than top horizontal
d) Protrusion ◯

For (3):
a) Has a left hook

8. Shapes
As shown

	(1)	(2)	(3)
9. Meaning:	cow	car	water
10. Sound:	niú	chē	shuǐ

11. Meaning of Vocabulary: [Name of place] **Chinatown in Singapore**

Strokes Bubble Map

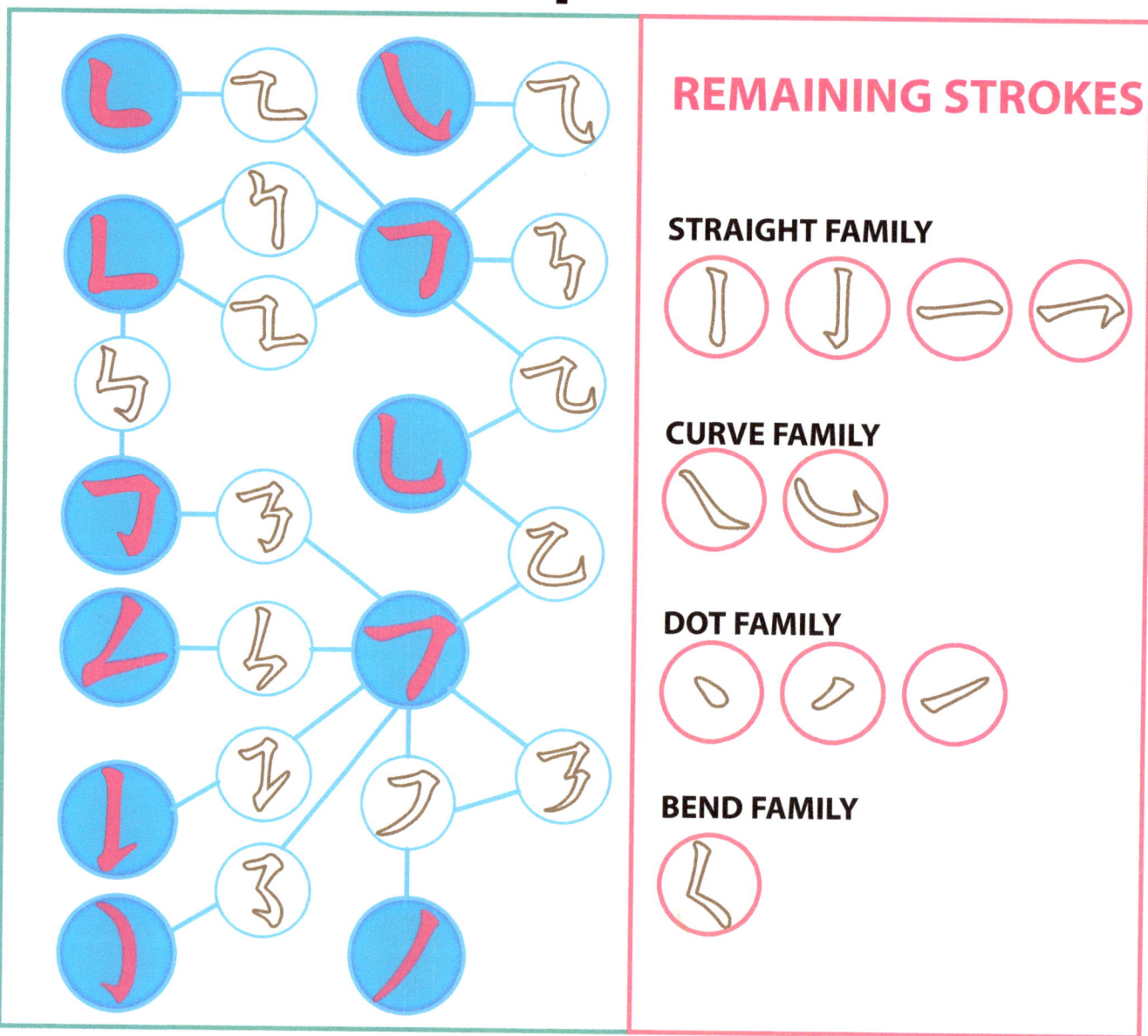

REMAINING STROKES

STRAIGHT FAMILY

CURVE FAMILY

DOT FAMILY

BEND FAMILY

Acknowledgement

This book is dedicated to my first Chinese language teacher—my father. I remember vividly how I was mesmerised by his 'calligraphy performance'. He would take out his favourite Parker ballpoint pen, straighten his posture, focus his gaze, carefully select the best spot on the paper and press the tip of the pen down firmly ... this was the start of a mini performance that I looked forward ... the tip of the pen moved gracefully across the paper ... slowing down a little on the last stroke of each character ... picking up speed again on the next character ... It was a breathtaking performance!

Handwritten Chinese characters are magically beautiful not only because of their appearance but also because of the process of writing them ... it is like dancing on the paper. There is so much grace, energy and rhythm, as well as freedom to express one's unique style. There is also techniques involved to ensure that the characters fall in line. A person who has excellent Chinese penmanship is regarded as someone who is educated, artistically-inclined, meticulous ...

So now can you see ... when I started learning Chinese, I was emotionally motivated, inspired to be a better person and challenged to be as good as my father. There was sensory stimulation ... immersing in calligraphy performances. There was no pressure to learn vocabularies, pronunciation, reading and other skills. These initial experiences made me love Chinese for what it is ... it is not a subject, it is not a tool, it is not for examinations, it is not for work ... it is just something that makes me feel good. I was in awe and felt challenged to master it.

Then why am I advocating *Learning Chinese Without Writing*?

Writing by hand seems to be an obsolete skill in this era with hardly any use for it. The ability to type accurately and quickly is more useful. Writing Chinese characters by hand is also such a tedious task that requires superior manual dexterity that young learners lack. Many young learners are so burdened by writing exercises that they feel that writing is a chore and complete them without giving much attention. Hence, as they learn more characters, they will become confused because the foundation of decoding characters stroke by stroke was not firmly laid. This seemingly time-consuming and mundane task of writing each character stroke by stroke pays off at a later stage of learning.

Even if it is beneficial to write by hand, the time required to complete these exercises is too much. How to reap the benefits of writing by hand and reduce the time required? Or rather how to make such tasks so enjoyable and beneficial that the time required is not a consideration. It can be part of play, part of art and craft, part of mathematics, part of creative problem solving . . . part of lifeskill (e.g. ability to spot differences). *Learn Chinese Without Writing* gives learners a choice to learn Chinese characters another way—visually. It creates a different learning experience for learners to fall in love with Chinese again.

This is my first book but it is not the first project that I embarked on to explore ways to learn Chinese effectively and innovatively. This content is introduced first because without this foundation, it will be difficult to introduce other books. It covers the fundamentals. Coincidentally, this is also a missing part in the whole field of Chinese learning.

It is disappointing that Chinese language materials are rarely creative. It really requires a lot of effort to think beyond the traditional ways of learning and teaching them. I am lucky to have grown up in a bilingual environment in Singapore where we have to learn English and Chinese since young. It provided the environment to compare the disparities between the teaching of these two subjects. The cognitive dissonance I experienced compelled me to explore beyond how I was taught and how Chinese could be taught.

This book is put together in a few months but it was really the culmination of years of exploration. All the content and activities in this book are original, never been published anywhere else. Instead of presenting them in text, I personally prefer to present them in visuals with only a short description if needed.

More interesting content will be introduced in subsequent books. Each of them will be an innovation by itself and may even be a disruption to the current way of teaching Chinese.

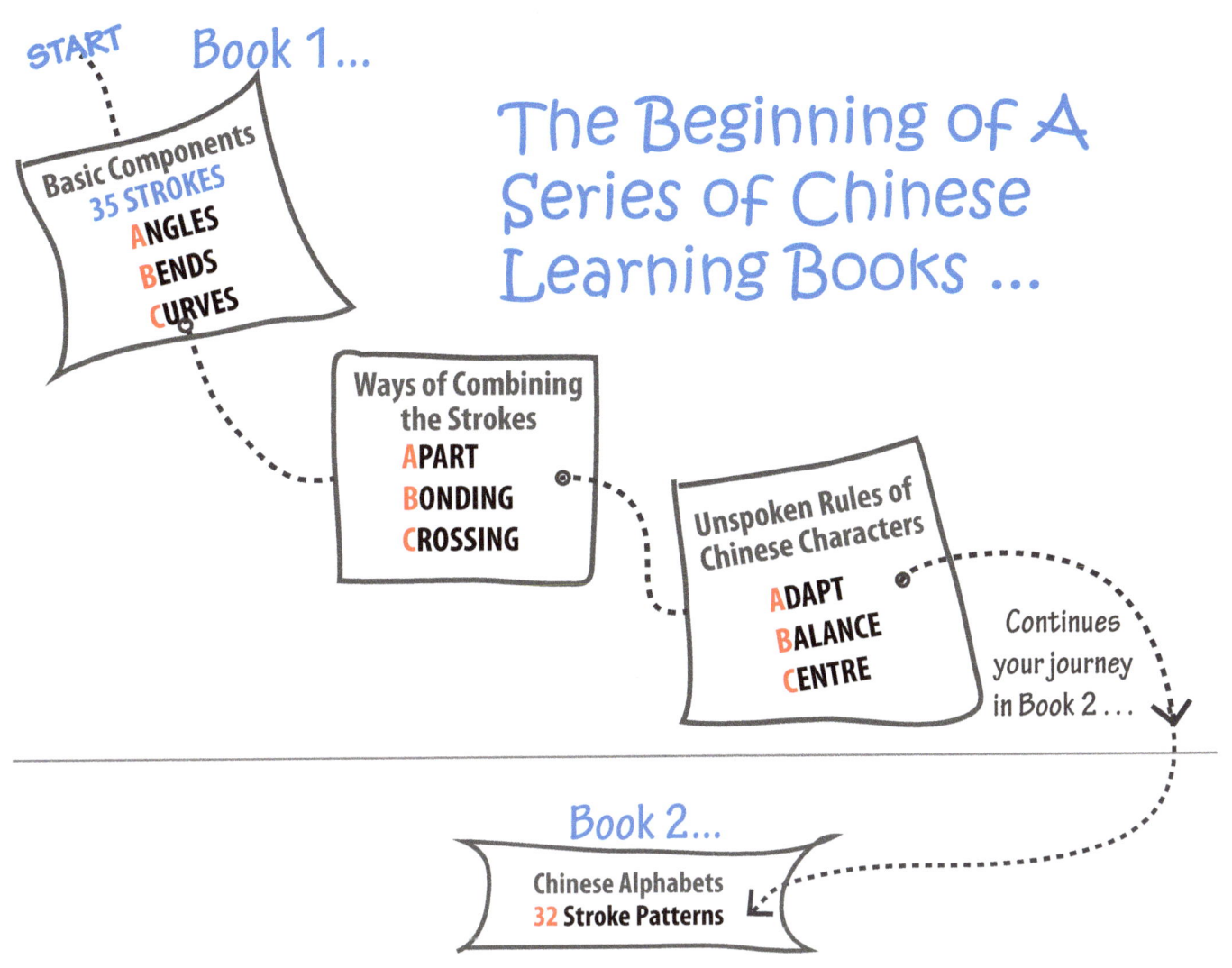

START

Book 1...

Basic Components
35 STROKES
ANGLES
BENDS
CURVES

The Beginning of A Series of Chinese Learning Books ...

Ways of Combining the Strokes
APART
BONDING
CROSSING

Unspoken Rules of Chinese Characters
ADAPT
BALANCE
CENTRE

Continues your journey in Book 2 ...

Book 2...

Chinese Alphabets
32 Stroke Patterns

Preview of Book 2

Decode simplified Chinese characters after knowing just 32 stroke patterns!

Learn a few hundred parts instead of thousands of characters!

Save a lot of time and effort!

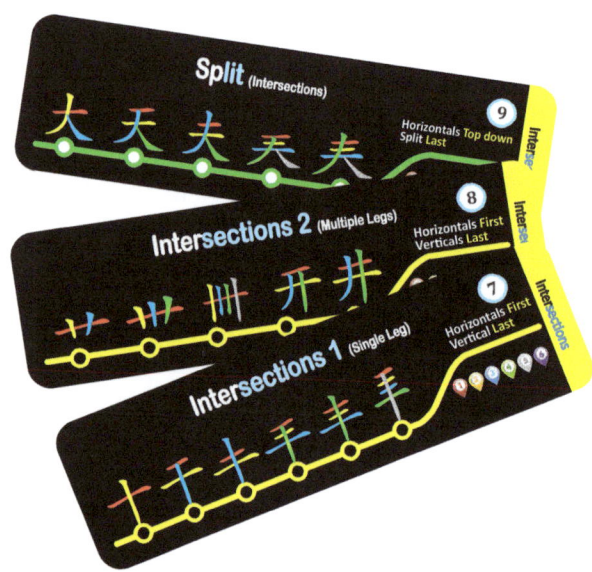

Contact:
Email: wqblosh@gmail.com

Art & Craft 1

Cut out this page and create a symmetrical character. See instructions next page.

xǐ

(verb) *like, be happy*
(noun) *happy occasion*

like

be happy

happy occasion

2. Fold along line and cut out all the white portions.

Art & Craft 2

Cut out this page and create a symmetrical character. See instructions next page.

xǐ

*(noun) **double happiness***

double happiness

double happiness

double happiness

double happiness

double

happiness

2. Fold along line and cut out all the white portions.